DIW BERLIN

4

AF833517

Vierteljahrshefte zur Wirtschaftsforschung 4.2021

Finance Meets Sustainability: A New Hope?

Duncker & Humblot · Berlin

DIW Berlin – Deutsches Institut
für Wirtschaftsforschung e. V.

Mohrenstraße 58, 10117 Berlin
Tel. +49-30-8 97 89-0
Fax +49-30-8 97 89-200
www.diw.de

SALE AND DISTRIBUTION
VERLAG DUNCKER & HUMBLOT GMBH
Carl-Heinrich-Becker-Weg 9
12165 Berlin

DESIGN
Edenspiekermann

LAYOUT AND COMPOSITION
3w+p GmbH, Rimpar

PRINT
2022 bei CPI buchbücher.de gmbh, Birkach

Printed in Germany

Printed on FSC-certified paper

ISSN 0340-1707 (Print) / 1861-1559 (Online)
ISBN 978-3-428-18652-5

Editorial: Finance Meets Sustainability: A New Hope?

MECHTHILD SCHROOTEN, ARMIN VARMAZ AND DOROTHEA SCHÄFER

Mechthild Schrooten, Hochschule Bremen, e-mail: mechthild.schrooten@hs-bremen.de
Armin Varmaz, School of International Business Bremen, e-mail: armin.varmaz@hs-bremen.de
Dorothea Schäfer, DIW Berlin & Jönköping University, e-mail: dschaefer@diw.de

Sustainability has climbed up the international agenda of governments and businesses over the past decade. The United Nations Sustainable Development Goals (SDGs), for example, cover 17 areas that address critical global issues such as hunger, extreme poverty, disease, social inequality and climate change and the SDGs should be achieved by 2030. Achieving the SDGs will require large public and private sector investments. Estimates of the level of investment required range from \$1.7 trillion to \$8 trillion per year, which equals 2 % to 9 % of global GDP per year.

Financial intermediaries, investors, professionals and stakeholders are involved in several ways to deliver on SDGs:

- as investors providing capital for sustainable investments,
- as developers of financial products focused on sustainable developments, and
- as stakeholders being exposed to sustainable risks.

Sustainable development includes both opportunities (e. g., distributing new sustainable financial products) and risks (e. g., a borrower needing to decontaminate its soil) for the financial sector. In the U.S., risks to banks increased through a series of lawsuits in the 1980s. The range of sustainability-focused activities is also evolving. For example, more so-called sustainable mutual funds are being offered to customers and carbon risks are being incorporated into financial assessments. Should the financial sector use its specific instruments to deliver on the SDGs? Does the financial sector need to base the investment and loan decision on sustainability ratios? To escape the traditional financial valuation, a shift in the current economic and social paradigm is needed.

The current issue of the *DIW Vierteljahrshefte zur Wirtschaftsforschung* directs attention to these questions. The issue includes selected papers from the conference "Sustainable Finance and Digitalization" jointly organized by DIW Berlin and the research cluster "Dynamics, tensions and Xtreme events" of the Hochschule Bremen.

The importance of the financial sector for achieving a sustainable development is significant. The financial sector transforms money into place, term, size and risk. Its influence is quantitative and qualitative, since the financial sector can determine which projects are funded, thus also affecting

Vierteljahrshefte zur Wirtschaftsforschung | DIW Berlin | volume 90 | 04.2021 | pages 5–6 the nature of financed projects. The financial sector can create funds that are specifically designed for investment in environmentally friendly ways, such as green funds. Applying a premium differentiation in line with the investment's degree of sustainability would be a further step in this direction. Accordingly, a specific investment or credit would then need to satisfy return or risk-management requirements that are in line with the financial institute's sustainability goals. The contributions in the current issue of the Vierteljahrshefte revolve around these topics. Specifically, the authors discuss the sustainability impact of divestment decisions, the measurement of real estate sustainability, the question of sustainable financial literacy, and green public procurement's impact on firm finance.

The first paper, "Sustainable Finance – Divestment as a Tool to Reach the SDGs?", by **Mechthild Schrooten** presents a critical review of the literature on sustainable divestment. Divestment is often seen as a popular strategy by investors to sanction harmful industries or socially not desired outcomes of economic activities. Schrooten shows that based on seminal theoretical work by Heinkel et al. (Heinkel, Kraus, & Zechner, 2001), divestment has limitations to deliver on SDGs. The current theory suggests that "voice" (engagement in the company) is superior to "exit" (divestment) in order to achieve the SDGs.

Janina Bösche highlights the importance of the real estate in achieving the SDGs in her paper "A Concept for Measuring Real Estate Sustainability from the Investors' Perspective". The real estate contributes 29 % to the EU greenhouse emission and it consumes 40 % of the EU energy. She proposes a concept for developing a real estate sustainability metric and presents specific sustainability indicators for the real estate sector. The aim is twofold: to add the non-financial indicators to the real estate evaluation and to assess sustainability risks from the perspective of investors.

The paper "Sustainable Financial Literacy and Preferences for Sustainable Investments among Young Adults", by **Armin Varmaz**, **Katharina Riebe** and **Sabrina Hegner**, sheds new light on the question of which preferences young adults have for sustainable investments. Their findings suggest that the environment focus is more important for the choice of sustainable investment than social or governance aspects. Latent behavioral characteristics (conscientiousness, importance of the impact of direct investments on sustainability, risk aversion, financial literacy) are also important to explain the young adults' choice of sustainable funds.

The final paper of this issue is on "Firms in Green Public Procurement: Financial Strength Indicators' Impact on Contract Awards and Its Repercussion on Financial Strength" by **Christopher Baum**, **Arash Kordestani**, **Dorothea Schäfer**, and **Andreas Stephan**. It examines whether the financial strength of companies is causally linked to the award of a public procurement contract, especially in the "green" area. The work is part of the XPRESS project which received funding from the European Union's Horizon 2020 Research and Innovation programme. Their results suggest that a lower equity ratio and a higher short-term debt ratio increase the probability of being successful in a public tender and that the companies can operate after the award with a lower equity ratio than comparable companies without an award, regardless of whether the company was successful in a traditional or a "green" public tender. They conclude from their findings that success in a public procurement contract may certify a firm's future earning strength, thus facilitating better access to external financing.

Sustainable Finance – Divestment as a Tool to Reach the SDGs?

MECHTHILD SCHROOTEN

Mechthild Schrooten, Hochschule Bremen, e-mail: mechthild.schrooten@hs-bremen.de

Abstract: This paper synthesizes the literature on sustainable divestment. Nowadays, divestment seems to be a popular strategy to sanction harmful industries or socially not desired outcomes of economic activities. However, in practice for a long time many firms which were known for harmful technologies did not face divestment or a loss in value. Seminal theoretical work was done by Heinkel et al. (Heinkel, Kraus, & Zechner, 2001). Recent theoretical studies based on this approach show that divestment has huge limitations. Theory explains that "voice" (engagement in the company) is superior to "exit" (divestment).

Nevertheless, the divestment movement and campaigns are of considerable social size. The effects of divestment on the financial market seems to be small in monetary terms. However, there are a lot of side effects, such increasing social awareness concerning the wasteful lifestyle. The divestment movement is gaining importance and actors. Therefore, the divestment movement is a supporting tool to reach SDGs. Not directly via the impact on the financial market, but by raising the social awareness.

Zusammenfassung: Dieses Papier bereitet die gängige Literatur zum Thema „Divestment" auf. Über eine lange Zeit konnten viele Firmen, die für den Einsatz umweltschädlicher Technologien bekannt waren, lange Zeit davon ausgehen, dass sie nicht über den Finanzmarkt sanktioniert werden. Heutzutage scheint Divestment eine verbreitete Strategie zu sein, um umweltschädliche Unternehmensaktivitäten zu sanktionieren. Grundlegende theoretische Arbeiten zum Thema Divestment wurden von Heinkel et al. (Heinkel, et al., 2001) veröffentlicht. Jüngste theoretische Studien, die auf diesem Ansatz basieren, zeigen, dass die Wirtksamkeit von Divestment begrenzt ist. Vielmehr scheint „Voice" (Engagement im Unternehmen) dem „Exit" (Divestment) überlegen zu sein.

In der Praxis jedoch stoßen die Divestment-Kampagnen auf eine beachtliche gesellschaftliche Resonanz. Die Auswirkungen von Divestment auf den Finanzmarkt scheinen dagegen eher gering zu sein. Es gibt jedoch viele indirekte Effekte von Divestment, wie z. B. ein zunehmendes gesellschaftliches Bewusstsein für den umweltschädliche Unternehmenspolitik und Konsumgewohnheiten. Daher kann Divestment als indirektes wirkendes Instrument zur Erreichung der SDGs betrachtet werden. Divestment entwickelt demnach seine Strahlkraft nicht direkt über die Auswirkungen auf den Finanzmarkt, sondern durch die Sensibilisierung der Gesellschaft.

→ JEL classification: G11, Q54, B59
→ Keywords: Investment Decisions, Divestment, Campaigns, CO_2 reduction

1 Introduction

The so-called Sustainable Development Goals (SDGs) are rather fundamental, challenging and revolutionary. Despite the fact that the member states of the United Nations are heterogenous in many respects, all of them adopted a common set of goals for a sustainable future in 2015. The SDGs are covering a wide range of topics – from "no poverty" over "zero hunger" to "climate action". Basically, the SDGs address different harmful consequences of capitalism and market failures.

Most of the 17 Sustainable Development Goals (SDGs) can be easily linked to finance. Their realization requires a certain allocation of financial resources. Some of the goals can be reached only by innovation. Innovation means not only invention of new technologies. Innovation means divestment in traditional technologies, too. This might be reflected in additional costs for companies and consumers – and might drive inflation. The SDGs are getting more important for companies by the increasing public interest in the incorporation of environmental, social and governance (ESGs) considerations of the different industries. There exists a huge rating industry for ESGs criteria (Escrig-Olmedo, et al., 2019). The SDGs are closely related not only to the ESGs but also to the field of sustainable, responsible and impact investment (SRI).

Especially, responsible consumption and production (SDG goal number 12) and climate action (goal number 13) gained attention over the last decade. To reach the goal "responsible consumption and production" not only investment in adequate technologies is requires, but there seems to be a need for a more fundamental change. By this a new and commonly used indicator for harmful economic actions emerged: the Co2 emission. Responsible investment means investment with zero Co2 and can be distinguished from irresponsible investment with high CO_2 emissions. Nevertheless, the EU commission defines sustainable finance in a broader sense: "Sustainable finance refers to the process of taking *environmental, social and governance (ESG) considerations* into account when making investment decisions in the financial sector, leading to more long-term investments in sustainable economic activities and projects" (European Commission, 2022). Responsible consumption – in this context – can be defined in the same way as responsible investment (United Nations, 2022). Within this context, the terms "responsible and "sustainable" is used synonymously.

Here, we focus on just one aspect of sustainability: CO_2 emissions. In practice, over the last decade CO_2 emissions have become a profile issue for many firms. In 2015 the binding Paris Agreement was signed by 195 nations. This agreement ends the long period of free carbon dioxide pollution. By addressing the climate change via pricing, governments end the long period of costless externalities by CO_2 emissions for both, consumers and producers. At the core of this agreement there is the "goal is to *limit global warming* to well below 2, *preferably to 1.5 degrees Celsius*, compared to pre-industrial levels" (United Nations, 2022). CO_2 emission go back to a huge degree to fossil fuel industries.

Regulation and governmental interventions are gaining power, in both the academic and the political sphere. The last decades made it clear: Neoliberal assumptions on the healing powers of markets might be fulfilled in a world of perfect markets – but not in a reality. Market failures are part of the existing economic systems. With both, the SDGs and the Paris Agreement it can be argued that we are at the eve of a new legal framework for all business models. This step does not result from the market, neither from global firms – it results only from the changes in (international) regulation and the cooperation of governments. Thus, it results from global environmental policies. What is the role of investors and the international financial market in this setting?

All in all not only for the activist movement but also for responsible financial investors many questions arise: (1) What is the recent size of divestment? (2) What is the social impact of divestment? (3) Do financial investors have a chance for signaling? (4) Can divestment result in socially desired outcomes? (5) Is the financial market responsible for signals, or is the regulation? Here, we offer a literature-based study on the size and the success factors of divestment focusing on fossil fuel divestment. Fossil fuel consumption and production is closely linked to the general SDGs and the ESG considerations of companies and is one of the major concerns for the future development.

2 Background – Stylized Facts

The history of divestment seems to be as old as the one of investment. Basically, we can distinguish between the strategic decision of a company for divestment and the financial market evaluation of this decision. In an early study Durhaime and Grant (1984) come to the result that firms which decide for divestment are in relatively weak position compared to their competitors (Durhaime & Grant, 1984). Thus, from the perspective of a firm divestment is an indicator for weakness. Divestment can be part of the foreign direct investment decisions. With divestment firms are focusing on their core business. However, this kind of divestment goes back to strategic decisions. If the divestment is part of the overall strategy Montgomery et al. come to the result that this leads to a positive development of the stock market (Montgomery, Thomas, & Kamath, 1984). Both findings can be compromised to: divestment occurs in times of low performance and leads in some cases to a gain of market value (Montgomery & Thomas, 1988). From the perspective of a firm divestment might lead to focusing on core and efficient operations and production.

However, modern divestment is more than just moving money from one sector to the other for generating higher profits. Today, socially responsible investment and divestment is a hot topic. Activist investors want to prevent harmful production, injustice or political unrest. The sustainable investor wants to reach a socially desirable result – not just profits. By this, divestment might be closely linked to the questions of corporate social responsibility (CSR) (Kitzmueller & Shimshack, 2012). However, there are many differences since CSR covers a broad range of activities (Schoenmarker & Schramade, 2019). Sustainability or CO_2 reduction is only one of the large set of topics. In general, it can be assumed that CSR addresses sustainability issues from a strategic perspective of a company in the long-term (Christensen, Hail, & Leuz, 2019). Christensen et al. show the huge differences in measuring CSR activities by ESG-rating agencies. These conceptual differences make it difficult to compare the results – this signaling for the financial market is rather diffuse.

CSR activities might be in line with the shareholders' interests, it can increase the value of a firm. However, CSR gives the firm a purpose broader than profit or market value maximization. Basically, we can distinguish between voluntary and mandatory CSR activities of firms. The mandatory CSR activities have to be published in CSR reports, which offer information to both, investors and consumers. According to the literature, different CSR activities can lead to mixed results with respect to the firm's value or profit (Christensen, Hail, & Leuz, 2019).

Financial investment is closely linked to buying shares on the stock exchange. The shareholders are partial owners of company. Partial ownership is linked to a proportional voting right. Multinational companies are issuing a large number of shares. Typically, the influence of each individual shareholder on the decision making of the firm is neglectable. Thus, in practice only large groups of investors with a common interest or institutional investors such as pension funds or (large) investment funds might be able for significant divestment. From the perspective of the responsible investor divestment is part of her shareholder's strategies. In recent times shareholders might have preferences for goals such as CO_2 reductions even at the expense of profits. Consequently, divestment seems to be a popular strategy to sanction harmful industries or socially not desired outcomes of economic activities.

Figure 1

Divestment: A simple idea

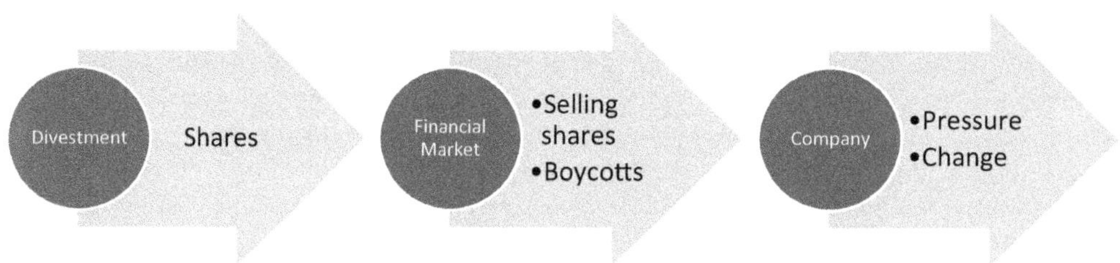

Source: Own.

The decision for divestment goes not only back to moral reasons. It is supported by growing risk of harmful investments. However, the increasing risk of harmful technologies is well reported since many years. Nevertheless, for a long period of time this kind of operational risk was not priced in the financial market. The World Bank provides examples about the scope of environmental harmful investments, nearly all traditional industries are affected (The World Bank, 2017).

3 Theory: What Does the Literature Tell?

Even within traditional neoliberal theoretical models CO_2 emissions are considered as negative externalities. For a long period of time these emissions were not priced. By changing this private investment decisions have to be revaluated. In addition, nowadays, investment and divestments in environmentally objectionable companies are attracting a lot of public attention – not only in the media but on the financial market. The fossil fuel divestment campaign is an important example for the increasing moral and political power of financial funds and investors (e.g. McKibben, 2018). From the perspective of companies and investors which are engaged in an objectionable project this might induce an asset price shock – or a stop of credit lines. From the perspective of a potential investor the engagements in such industries is getting riskier. The divestment movement is focusing on the financial market. However, the buying and selling shares of the company on the stock market are rarely financing a firm (Orr, 2022). At the moment of the "initial public offering" (IPO) of share the company is getting directly fresh money from the market. After IPO the shares are traded on the stock market without a direct effect on the financial situation of a given firm.

However, indirectly the stock price of the share will influence the access of the company to additional financial resources, such as loans or successfully issued bonds.

Most of the theoretical literature on divestment is focusing on the case that the potential investor is buying shares. Typically, it is assumed that there are there are at least two different groups of investors – selfish investors (not aware of ESGs) and investors with social preferences (aware of ESGs). It seems to be trivial that as long as the group of selfish investors is large enough, the investors with social preferences will not succeed. This goes back to the fact, that the strength of the voice of the socially responsible investor is proportional to the value of the asset invested. In the seminal work of Heinkel et al. it is shown that the impact of divestment is not proportional to the value of the asset (Heinkel, Kraus, & Zechner, 2001)! There is always the risk, that the seize of divestment is too small to be significant for the decision making within the firm. In addition, Heinkel et al. show that profit seeking investors act as a substitute for divested capital.

In their more recent theoretical paper Broccari et al. analyze the welfare effects of divestments (exit). They compare it to the effects of active engagement of investors in the firm ("voice"). Basically, it is assumed that a higher degree of environmental consciousness leads to higher costs for the firm and thus lower profits and monetary benefits for the shareholder (Broccardo, Hart, & Zingales, 2020). According to the model, clean investment makes only sense if the ecological damage of production is higher than the additional fixed cost of firm. In addition, Broccari et al. assume that the welfare effect of this decision is influenced by the weight of preferences for green investment λ of the individual investor. To a certain degree, their model is an augmentation of the Heinkel et al. paper (Hart & Zingales, 2017). This strand of literature is taking the individual preference for sustainable production as a public good. Thus, there are high incentives for free-riding – the burden for sustainable investment would be covered only by responsible investors, anyway. Within such a model, the welfare effect of the divestment decision of a single investor is neglectable (marginal effects). Furthermore, there might be a difference between individual and social preferences for divestment. According to this arithmetic model, at least two interesting situations might occur: (1) There could be the one pivotal marginal investor being responsible for a change of the whole investment process. (2) Regulation (the authors call it "the benevolent planner") could devaluate harmful technologies. In such a case the question arises to what degree clean technologies are required by the regulator. It can be shown that the decision of existing firms to invest in new "clean" technologies depends on the difference between (fixed) cost for new investment and the cost for damage. The whole model can be summarized as follows: The success of divestment ("exit") depends on the intensity of preferences for divestment, the cost of clean technology and the cost of ecological damage. According to this class of models, regulation is much more effective than divestment. In addition, the authors show that "voice" is more effective than divestment. By this they support the ideas of Hirschman that in general investors have to decide between "exit" and engagement ("voice") the organization. Hirschman argued that "voice" as strategy to change the behavior of the organization is superior (Hirschman, 1970).

A second strand of literature is analyzing the impact of divestment on the financial performance of a firm. Oehmke et al. show that: "Impact requires a broad mandate, in that socially responsible investors need to internalize social costs irrespective of whether they are investors in a given firm. Impact is optimally achieved by enabling a scale increase for clean production." (Oehmke & Opp, 2020). Taking a similar approach as Brocarro et al. the authors focus on "voice" rather than on radical divestment. According to Oehmke et al. socially responsible investors could act effectively by financing the clean investment of a firm. Within such models it usually assumed that "clean" investment is "expensive" investment and reduces the profit of a given firm. The authors distinguish between financial investors and socially responsible investors. Basically, underinvestment in clean investments is one important precondition for a successful cooperation between financial and social investors. The other is that the damage generated by the firm attracts the action of social investors. From the perspective of the socially responsible investor the preference for a single firm depends on a Social Profitability Index (SPI) which is ranking the firms. It is assumed that the socially responsible investor is confronted with scarcity of capital. Thus, there is a selection process and the firm selected by the responsible investor must fulfill minimum conditions to be attractive for social investment. As Brocorro et al. Oehmke et al. show that divestment is less effective than engagement from the perspective of the socially responsible investor.

A different approach is taken by Lagandier and Lovo (2020). The authors consider the effects of an ESG funds on financing. It is assumed that funds are maximizing market size, firms are maximizing profit and investors are maximizing returns. The authors show that in such a world the ESG funds has an impact on the investment decision. According to their argumentation the funds would be engaged in harmful firms and support them to shift to green technologies. Again, as in the models mentioned above engagement of funds is important for the implementation of green technologies (Landier & Stefano, 2020).

All in all, this kind of recent theoretical literature shows a huge tendency to support the view that divestment is a less effective strategy. According to these papers a change to a green world needs investment which is more expensive than traditional investment. This is why the socially responsible investor is so important. Based on her preferences she is willing to accept a lower return on investment.

4 Empirical Considerations

Is divestment or engagement of responsible investors is more sufficient to reach socially desired outcomes? Several existing theoretical papers on divestment are focusing on this question. Usually, it can be shown that the most efficient tool to reach sustainable development is regulation. This fact is well known in practice, too. However, regulation is often lagging. Some authors argue that we are not only confronted with market failures, but policy failures too (Broccardo, Hart, & Zingales, 2020).

Some of the papers combine theoretical considerations with empirics. In the seminal work of Heinkel et al. a larger set of firms is taken the impact of divestment is analyzed. Nowadays, there is a public movement of activists all around the world voting for divestment. An increasing number of campaigns are advocating for sustainable investment the and divestment from companies with harmful production technologies. Some activist even put their lives on social justice and see intervention in financial markets an appropriate tool to foster the change (Orr, 2022). These movements are strong in western societies. They could gain power by cumulative effects and the size of the funds– however often the indirect effects on sustainability are neglected (Ritchie & Dowlatabali, 2014). Those campaigns are often lacking from distinguishing between divestment and defunding. Since only defunding is limiting the financial resources of the company. However, in terms of public consciousness the divestment movement in western societies can be called a success. In the next section we take a look at the campaigns which can be considered as to part of the overall fossil fuel divestment movement.

4.1 Divestment: Actors

The divestment idea is promoted by a broad set of actors. Today, campaigns for climate protection are part of the overall social, economic and political life. The idea of climate protecting divestment campaigns gained power after activist Bill McKibben published his article on climate math in the Rolling Stone 2012 (McKibben, 2012). A broad climate justice movement was born and supported by McKibben's 350.org platform. The platform explains its goals: "(1) A fast & just transition to 100 % renewable energy for all, (2) No new fossil fuel projects anywhere and (3) Not a penny more for dirty energy" (350.org, 2022). At least goal 3 is closely linked to divestment. In recent days, the goals of the divestment campaigns were not only shared by activists by also by organizations like pension funds and profit- oriented companies.

The database on Global Fossil Fuel Divestment (https://divestmentdatabase.org/) gives an impression about the size of this kind of divestment (Figure 2). The database explains that today the size of fossil fuel divestment is about 40 trillion USD by 1507 institutions. Since 2014 the size of divestment has grown by 75 percent. This might go back to achievements in the context of the Paris Agreement. Interestingly, the largest share of the overall amount goes back to faith-based organizations[1] followed by educational institutions. The 2021 report on fossil fuel divestment explains: "Major new divestment commitments from iconic institutions have arrived in a rush over just a few months in late 2021, including Harvard University, Dutch and Canadian pension fund giants PME and CDPQ, French public bank La Banque Postale, the U.S. city of Baltimore, and the Ford and MacArthur Foundations." (Global Divestment Comittment Database, 2021)

Today the divestment movement is gaining public interest and speed. However, a decade ago divestment seemed to be not attractive. CO_2 emissions were not priced. Thus, the industries could realize externalities at a zero cost. Only in the more recent time, pricing and shifts in the legal framework put some cost on CO_2 emissions. From the perspective of an investor rising costs or legal bans are increasing the risk. By, this a certain endogeneity of less or non-investment occurs, even in a fully-fledged financial market economy. Even within this framework it does not make huge sense to invest in markets which undermine the living conditions on the planet.

Pollin and Hansen are offering a broad data set on fossil fuel divestment commitments (Hansen & Pollin, 2020). In the database about 800 organizations are listed. Today, the largest organizations committed to divestment are profit oriented companies (Table 1). Many of them committed to a certain field of divestment like coal.

At the beginning this divestment movement was focused on universities (Ayling & Gunningham, 2015). In the educational sector climate issues are addressed by implementing new standards like climate commitment for many years. By this most universities committed to carbon neutrality and developed zero waste programs, used environmentally friendly construction, implemented programs to saving energy, adopted sustainable purchasing policies and, and, and ... Additionally, many universities introduced new curricula or lectures addressing questions of climate change. According to the Global Divestment Database about 15 percent of the overall divestment activities go back to educational institutions – many of them are located in the US or in the United Kingdom.

1 One important advocate is Nobel prize winner Archebishop Tutu (Carrington, 2014). The fossil fuel divestment movement often refers to the experience of the apartheid divestment campaign in South Africa in the 70s and 80s.

Figure 2

Which institutional actors are divesting?

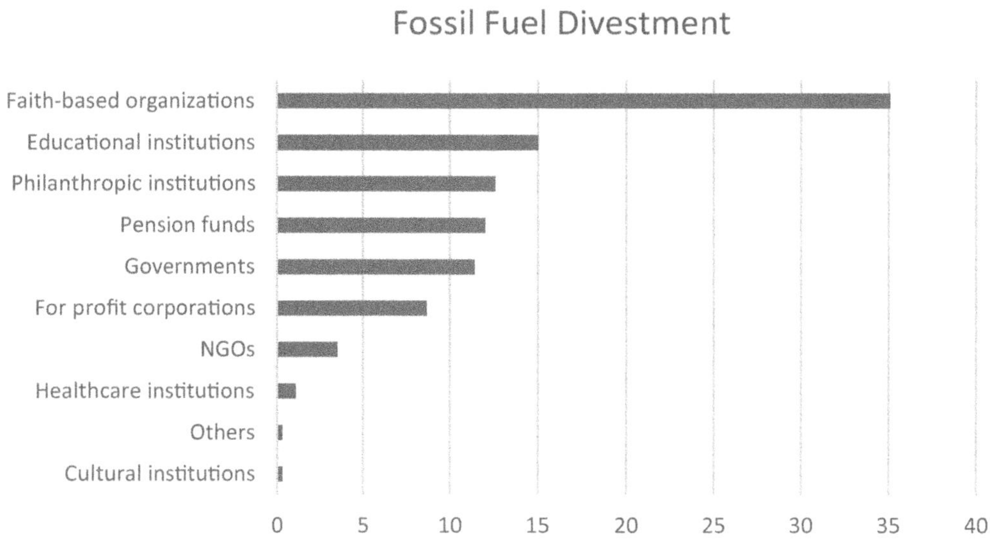

Source: Global divestment database.

Table 1

Who is divesting?

Rank	Name	Type	Country	Committment	Size – Billion USD
1	Government Pension Fund Global	Pension Fund	Norway	Coal Only	890
2	AXA I.M.	For Profit Corporation	France	Coal Only	782
3	Allianz SE	For Profit Corporation	Germany	Coal Only	668
4	AXA S.A.	For Profit Corporation	France	Coal Only	589
5	Aviva	For Profit Corporation	UK	Coal Only	572
6	Aegon N.V.	For Profit Corporation	Netherlands	Coal Only	382
7	Lloyd's	For Profit Corporation	UK	Coal Only	378
8	California Public Employees' Retirement System (CalPERS)	Pension Fund	USA	Coal Only	290
9	Nordea Asset Management	For Profit Corporation	Sweden	Coal Only	228
10	New York City Pension Fund System	Pension Fund	USA	Full	189

Source: Global Divestment Database.

The largest university participating is the University of California (98 billion USD) (Table 2). One very well-reported case is the American University's Fossil Free campaign (Bratman, Brunette, Shelly, & Nicolson, 2016). In their unconventional case study, the authors show that the result of the campaign the authors explain how this campaign has been affected by the questions of standards, market size and the decision between "voice" and "exit". The effects of the limiting factors the authors mention are more or less those factors which are considered as to be crucial in the theoretical literature on financial divestment. In addition, the authors mention one very important aspect of this campaign:

> "One thing that has become abundantly clear during the campaign is the extent to which a new generation of activists is eschewing older understandings of conservation and nature protection in favor of a growing focus on climate justice. This evolution of environmental activism has been much noted and certainly warrants greater attention. Climate change is becoming less abstract a notion as identifiable people and populations, visible to those in power, experience directly some of the impacts associated with a warming world. The FFAU campaign suggests that such experiences can drive people to move beyond important first steps like tackling personal energy consumption and move on to sustained, focused, and impactful political action" (Bratman, Brunette, Shelly, & Nicolson, 2016).

An interesting case is given by the Havard University which had a well noticed debate on the impact on divestment (Havard University, 2022). So far, the Havard University is not in the list of universities which claimed for divestment. The Havard University already at an early stage of movement encouraged for "voice" not for "exit" (for details: http://www.divestharvard.com/).

Table 2

Divestment – Universities

	Name	Country	Billion USD
1	University of California	USA	98
2	Yale University	USA	25,6
3	Stanford University	USA	22,1
4	University of Cambridge	UK	9,7
5	Birmingham City University	UK	6,6
6	Johns Hopkins University	USA	3,4
7	Oxford University	UK	2,6
8	University of Washington	USA	2,6
9	Boston University	USA	1,6
10	Georgetown University	USA	1,5

Source: Global Divestment Database.

4.2 How to Measure the Impact of Divestment?

Divestment is a non-governmental action. Modern divestment campaigns are transnational. However, the goal of the different climate related campaigns may differ. Therefore, it is difficult to measure the general impact of such campaigns. In general, it is reported that these campaigns contributed in many respects to the overall climate debate and the awareness of the SDGs. NGOs and campaigns are important for lobbying, consumer and investor education, shareholder engagement ("voice"), lobbying for the reduction of emissions, initiatives to introduce sustainable supply chain policies (boycotts, shaming), commitments to standards, such as certification regimes and voluntary principles. However, these different (transnational) campaigns do not have a common strategy or a common measurable goal (Ayling & Gunningham, 2015).

Especially, at the beginning the divestment movement developed fast and could a attract relatively huge investors not only from the educational sector. The financial *size* of listed actors in the Divestment Commitment Data set is considerable – however, compared to overall international financial market size it remains small.

Most of the important actors committed only to divest in just one industry: coal (Table 1). This might go back to the fact that today any investment in the coal industry is sanctioned by legal and *regulatory framework* and less attractive. Investment in the coal industry seems to be very risky. Divestment to coal seems to be part of a rational decision making. Thus, the membership in the list and the commitment would not have an extra effect on reaching the SDGs.

The *diversity of companies and institutions* which are committed to divestment is huge. Even institutions which earned their money from oil are on the list. One example is given by the Pension Fund from Norway, another example is given by the Rockefeller Fund (Size: 801 million USD). However, all these actors apply different definitions of what divestment means for them. It is not necessarily mean that they will sell all their shares which they own in just one moment.

Divestment campaigns *raise public interest*. Today the marketing effect of offering green products is huge. This might be one factor behind the membership of several well know large players on the list for commitment. Often these organizations choose only a soft-landing transformation process towards low emissions. A radical change in the supply-chain is usually not forseen. Only in the moment from which these organizations see that the risk to invest in such industries is to high they will change the business model. Thus, divestment might be even contra-productive as long as harmful industries can maximize profits.

The divestment movement was able to raise *the public consciousness* concerning climate change. It is important not only to explain the need to transition to a low-carbon economy as a matter of urgency, but also to link it to our recent lifestyle.

The divestment campaigns are not in vacuum – it is part of larger climate action movement. Some divestment initiatives make clear that a soft *transition* towards a market-oriented will not be possible. It is clear, what is not sustainable. However, what exactly is sustainable production in a market and profit-oriented society?

But is divestment the most effective way to reach CO_2 reduction? Even authors closely linked to the divestment movement come to result, the divestment is a long road and its effects are very complicated to analyze (Hansen & Pollin, 2018). The time is running and cannot be lost by long-term action plans. It can be easily shown, that as long as profit-seeking investors continue to see profit opportunities in owning fossil fuel industries they will investment and buy the shares offered by the divestment movement. Thus, for reaching the SDGs divestment has huge disadvantages, since it is not directly linked to funding of companies.

5 Conclusions

Divestment is a hot topic today. Sometimes divestment is considered to be similar to defunding. However, divestment is only selling shares or ownership rights. Selling ownership rights has not much in common with the idea of financing firms. Usually, the operations of firms financed by bonds, credits, cash-flow and only under extraordinary circumstances by issuing new shares.

Selling shares on the financial market is rather easy. If the responsible investor is selling the shares of fossil fuel company there is usually enough demand for those shares – as long as the company works profitable. Thus, externalities produced by the company cannot be addressed by divestment.

Only appropriate policies can help to price the externalities. As long as market failure is accompanied by policy failure and the price for the externalities is to low the financial market is the wrong address to reach socially responsible goals (Hansen & Pollin, 2018). Thus, there could be detected a strong ranking of strategies to reach and support the SDGs by movements. The best tool is regulation if this would be able to price any externalities. Regulation is binding and an accepted part of the "rules of the game" in a market economy. If policy is not able or willing to adjust the framework the second best solution will be "voice" – engagement within the system. Divestment is only weak tool to reach the SDGs.

Nevertheless, indirect effects of the divestment movement should not be neglected. The awareness of climate change and the need of appropriate policy measures is increasing. These "awareness"-effects already today influence policy actions – and by this in a second round the regulatory framework tends to be changed. However, these indirect effects take time which we do not have. Urgent action is required.

References

— 350.org. (2022): *About.* https://350.org/about/.
— Ayling, J. and N. Gunningham (2015, October): Non-state governance and climate policy: the fossil fuel divestment movement, pp. 131–149. https://www.tandfonline.com/doi/full/10.1080/14693062.2015.1094729?casa_token=LLvazlmvkH4AAAAA%3AgobLj1UKC_yBRz-Awmkwel3z_9380-XXhrGQ2myjYaxqxlZCTiL7ABGAK2Eii7F-xos19u0Hqnr5qw.
— Bratman, E., K. Brunette, D. C. Shelly, and S. Nicolson (2016, February): Justice is the goal: Divestment as climate change resistance. *Journal of Environmental Studies and Sciences,* pp. 677–690. https://link.springer.com/article/10.1007/s13412-016-0377-6.
— Broccardo, E., O. Hart, and L. Zingales (2020): *Exit vs Voice.* ECGI Working Paper.
— Carrington, D. (2014): Desmond Tutu calls for anti-apartheid style boycott of fossil fuel industry. *The Guardian.* https://www.theguardian.com/environment/2014/apr/10/desmond-tutu-anti-apartheid-style-boycott-fossil-fuel-industry.
— Christensen, H. B., L. Hail, and C. Leuz (2019): *Adoption of CSR and Sustainability Reporting Standards: Economic Analysis and Review.* Working Paper, BBER. https://www.nber.org/system/files/working_papers/w26169/revisions/w26169.rev0.pdf.
— Durhaime, I. M. and J. H. Grant (1984, October–December): Factors influencing the divestment decision-making. *Strategic Management Journal,* pp. 301–318. https://onlinelibrary.wiley.com/doi/10.1002/smj.4250050402.
— Escrig-Olmedo, E., M. A. Fernández-Izquierdo, I. Ferrero-Ferrero, J. M. Rivera-Lirio, and M. J. Muñoz-Torres (2019, February): Rating the Raters: Evaluating how ESG Rating. *Sustainability.* https://mdpi-res.com/d_attachment/sustainability/sustainability-11-00915/article_deploy/sustainability-11-00915-v2.pdf.
— European Commission (2022): *Overview of sustainable finance.* https://ec.europa.eu/info/business-economy-euro/banking-and-finance/sustainable-finance/overview-sustainable-finance_en.
— Global Divestment Comittment Database (2021): *Invest-Divest.* https://divestmentdatabase.org/wp-content/uploads/2021/10/DivestInvestReport2021.pdf.
— Hansen, T. and R. Pollin (2018): *Economics and Climate Justice Activism: Assessing the Fossil Fuel Divestment Movement.* PERI. https://peri.umass.edu/economists/robert-pollin/item/download/776_c9b3639c9a90abc599a4df058541cdbb.

— Hansen, T. and R. Pollin (2020): Data on Fossil Fuel Divestment Commitments through March 2018. *Data and Datasets 111*. https://scholarworks.umass.edu/data/111/.
— Hart, O. and L. Zingales (2017): Companies Should Maximize Shareholder Welfare Not Market Value. *Journal of Law, Finance, and Accounting*. https://www.nowpublishers.com/article/Details/LFA-0022.
— Havard University (2022): http://www.divestharvard.com/.
— Heinkel, R., A. Kraus, and J. Zechner (2001): The Effect of Green Investment on Corporate Behavior. *The Journal of Financial and Quantitative Analysis, 4*, pp. 431–449. https://www.jstor.org/stable/2676219.
— Hirschman, A. O. (1970): *Exit, Voice, and Loyalty: Responses to Decline in Firms, Organizations, and States*. Cambridge.
— Kitzmueller, M. and J. Shimshack (2012): Economic Perspectives on Corporate Social Responsibility. *Journal of Economic Literature, 1*, pp. 51–84. http://www.aeaweb.org/articles.php?doi=10.1257/jel.50.1.51.
— Landier, A. and L. Stefano (2020): Socially Responsible Finance: How to Optimize Impact. (H. R. Paper, Ed.) *1363*. https://papers.ssrn.com/sol3/papers.cfm?abstract_id=3508938.
— McKibben, B. (2012, July): Global Warming's Terrifying New Math. *The Rolling Stone*.
— McKibben, B. (2018): At last, divestment is hitting the fossil fuel. *The Guardian*. https://www.crcresearch.org/sites/default/files/imce/jclifton/At%20last%2C%20divestment%20is%20hitting%20the%20fossil%20fuel%20industry%20where%20it%20hurts%20%20Bill%20McKibben%20%20Opinion%20%20The%20Guardian.pdf.
— Montgomery, C. A. and A. R. Thomas (1988, Jan–Febr): Divestment: Motives and Gains, pp. 93–97.
— Montgomery, C. A., A. R. Thomas, and R. Kamath (1984): Divesture, market valuation and strategy. *Academy of Management Journal*, pp. 830–841.
— Oehmke, M. and M. M. Opp (2020): *A Theory of Socially Responsible Investment*. Research Paper, Swedish House of Finance. https://papers.ssrn.com/sol3/papers.cfm?abstract_id=3467644.
— Orr, D. (2022, January–February): Is Divestment Effective? Dollars *& Sense*, pp. 23–25.
— Pedersen, L. H., S. Fitzgibbons, and L. Pomorski (2019): *Responsible Investing: The ESG-Efficient Frontier*. https://papers.ssrn.com/sol3/papers.cfm?abstract_id=3466417.
— Ritchie, J. and H. Dowlatabali (2014, October): Understanding the shadow impacts of investment and divestment decisions: Adapting economic input–output models to calculate biophysical factors of financial returns. *Ecological Economics, 106*, pp. 132–140. https://www.sciencedirect.com/science/article/pii/S0921800914002079.
— Schoenmarker, D. and W. Schramade (2019): *Principles of Sustainable Finance*.
— The World Bank (2017): The Growing Role of Minerals and Metals for a Low Carbon Future. http://documents.worldbank.org/curated/en/207371500386458722/pdf/117581-WP-P159838-PUBLIC-ClimateSmartMiningJuly.pdf.
— United Nations (2022): *The 17 Goals*. https://sdgs.un.org/goals.
— United Nations (2022): *The Paris Agreement*. https://unfccc.int/process-and-meetings/the-paris-agreement/the-paris-agreement.

A Concept for Measuring Real Estate Sustainability from the Investors' Perspective

JANINA BÖSCHE

Janina Bösche, School of International Business Bremen, e-mail: Janina.Boesche@hs-bremen.de

Abstract: Although there is an increasing demand for sustainable investment products accompanied by increasing regulations regarding sustainability disclosures, people suffer from a lack of information concerning the offered investment products' sustainability. Despite hundreds of ESG indicators for standard investment products available in the literature, there is no holistic approach to assessing real estate sustainability to date. However, as the real estate sector is responsible for 40 % of energy consumption and 29 % of greenhouse gas emissions in the European Union, it is critical in meeting the Paris Agreement's climate targets. This paper presents our ideas for developing a concept for a real estate sustainability metric and real estate specific sustainability indicators. We aim to develop a metric that offers a transparent sustainability assessment for real estate based on the triple bottom line, thereby enabling (potential) investors to assess the sustainability of offered assets for themselves.

Zusammenfassung: Obwohl die Nachfrage nach nachhaltigen Anlageprodukten steigt und die Regulierung zur Offenlegung von Nachhaltigkeitsaspekten zunimmt, mangelt es auf Seiten der Anleger:innen an Informationen über die Nachhaltigkeit der angebotenen Anlageprodukte. Auch wenn in der Literatur hunderte von ESG-Indikatoren für Standard-Investmentprodukte zur Verfügung stehen, gibt es bisher keinen ganzheitlichen Ansatz zur Bewertung der Nachhaltigkeit von Immobilien. Da der Immobiliensektor jedoch für 40 % des Energieverbrauchs und 29 % der Treibhausgasemissionen in der Europäischen Union verantwortlich ist, ist er für die Erreichung der Ziele des Pariser Klimaabkommens von entscheidender Bedeutung. In diesem Artikel stellen wir unsere Ideen zur Entwicklung eines Konzepts für eine Nachhaltigkeitsmetrik für Immobilien und immobilienspezifische Nachhaltigkeitsindikatoren vor. Unser Ziel ist es, eine Metrik zu entwickeln, die eine transparente Nachhaltigkeitsbewertung für Immobilien auf der Grundlage des Drei-Säulen-Modells bietet und damit (potenzielle) Investor:innen in die Lage versetzt, die Nachhaltigkeit der angebotenen Assets selbst zu bewerten.

→ JEL classification: G11, Q51, R11
→ Keywords: Real Estate Sustainability, ESG Score, Asset Evaluation

1 Introduction

Sustainability seems to be on everyone's lips. Individuals are increasingly asking for sustainable products in all sectors (German Federal Environmental Agency "Umweltbundesamt" 2021). In addition, the demand for sustainable investment products has increased rapidly. From 2019 to 2020, investments in sustainable investment products increased by 124.5%, while the overall volume of investment products increased by only 10.7% (BVI 2021, p. 1; FNG 2021, p. 22). This increased demand is also evident in the real estate sector (EY 2021, p. 1). Although more and more people are willing to invest in sustainable products, they suffer from a lack of information regarding the sustainability of the offered investment products (Consumer Advice Centre "Verbraucherzentrale" 2021). In the context of real estate specifically, tools to measure sustainability are missing (Plößl and Just 2020, p. 23; Vieira de Castro et al. 2020, p. 267).

This paper aims to present the development of a concept for a real estate sustainability metric and real estate specific sustainability indicators that enable (potential) investors to assess the sustainability of offered assets for themselves. Several sustainability indicators are aggregated into categories before one final score is determined. The value added of having one total sustainability score is its signaling function. It provides investors with a brief overview of a potential investment's sustainability, while still offering them a more detail-oriented view of each investment through each indicator. In contrast to, e.g., the balanced scorecard or the Common Good Balance Sheet,[1] which are tools for the internal performance measurement of companies, our concept is primarily conceived to enable investors to assess their (potential) investments in real estate. We will only focus on buildings for this article and exclude land. We use the word "metric" for a system of weighted sustainability indicators. "Sustainability indicators" in this article are measures for single aspects of sustainability in the context of real estate, e.g., "women directors". A "category" is defined as a bundle of weighted sustainability indicators, e.g., "diversity".

For our metric, the triple bottom line serves as the basic concept. For the sustainability indicators, we determine relative measures to make our metric applicable to real estate globally, following a multi-step procedure (an algorithm), instead of one formula. These measures are based on scores instead of the binary system, which is the predominant measure for certificates (Rogmans and Ghunaim 2016, p. 607; Vieira de Castro et al. 2020). Scores instead of binary measures are necessary to make the extent and the specific way of sustainability recognizable. Our metric and sustainability indicators aim at providing investors with a transparent sustainability evaluation through a flexible and straightforward analysis. This allows investors to independently check whether the real estate of interest meets their own sustainability preferences. In addition, investors can assess whether their preferences regarding the magic pyramid of sustainable investment (return, risk, liquidity, and sustainability) are considered by investing in real estate. Furthermore, investors can use the metric to assess the current sustainability of their real estate and the potential sustainability risks.

Moreover, applying our metric is simpler than certifications and requires neither expert knowledge nor much time because all sustainability indicators are compiled in one clearly arranged checklist. Therefore, investors no longer need to rely on how private or public organizations assess and probably certify the sustainability of real estate assets. Instead, they can form their own judgment

1 https://www.ecogood.org/apply-ecg/sustainable-development-goals/.

with the help of our metric. The mechanism will be made publicly available online for free. Our contribution to the literature is developing a concept that provides a transparent and holistic assessment of the sustainability of real estate taking into account its whole lifecycle.

The article is structured as follows: Section 2 explains the peculiarities of the real estate sector and real estate as an asset. Section 3 provides an overview of the existing research and practical approaches. Section 4 details the concept, starting with the system boundaries, before discussing the development of sustainability indicators and their weighting and aggregation to categories. Section 4 concludes by discussing the sustainability score, ensuing ranking of the resulting scores, and the validation of the concept. The article ends with a conclusion in section 5, which summarizes the most important aspects and identifies both limitations of the results and recommendations for further research.

2 The Special Need of the Real Estate Sector for Sustainability Measurement

In addition to the increased demand for sustainable investment products, an important driver for needing to establish sustainability indicators is increasing regulation, which is supposed to have a long-term impact on the real estate industry (PwC and the Urban Land Institute 2020, p. 81; Bienert 2016, p. 16). As an example, the Taxonomy Regulation of the European Union imposes additional reporting obligations (European Commission 2019). The German Federal Financial Supervisory Authority "BaFin" published the Guidance Notice on Dealing with Sustainability Risks in January 2020 (German Federal Financial Supervisory Authority "BaFin" 2020). In March 2021, the European Disclosure Regulation came into force, according to which, financial companies must prove how sustainable their offerings are (European Union 2019). Additionally, carbon pricing will result in additional costs for real estate owners and, thus, a loss of return for those owners with less sustainable real estate properties (German Federal Government 2020; Spanner and Wein 2020, p. 289). Regulations regarding money laundering are continuously strengthened as well, such as through the Fifth Money Laundering Directive, which has been transposed into German law through an amendment of the Money Laundering Act in 2020 or the conversion of the Transparency Register in August 2021 to a full register, which, among other things, provides data on beneficial owners of real estate properties (European Union 2018; German Federal Ministry of Finance "Bundesfinanzministerium" 2020, 2021; Bausch and Voller 2020, p. 10 ff.). Finally, in May 2021, the European Union established the European Labour Authority, a permanent platform to tackle undeclared work (European Labour Authority 2021).

For the real estate sector and its related investment products, being part of the change toward more sustainability is of particular importance:

1. From an environmental perspective, the real estate sector has a significant impact, as it is responsible for 40 % of energy consumption and 29 % of greenhouse gas emissions within the European Union (Spanner and Wein 2020, p. 278). Additionally, it is very resource intensive. Due to the real estate's long lifecycle, resources – once consumed – are tied up for the long term.
2. In addition, the real estate sector has a special social role: On the one hand, humans need real estate to satisfy their basic need of housing. On the other hand, the real estate sector is

particularly susceptible to economic crime, such as illicit work and money laundering (German Federal Criminal Police Office 2012, p. 15).

3. Furthermore, the real estate sector has an exposed economic position because it generates 18.2% of Germany's gross domestic product; 25.1% of German companies and 9.5% of German employees work in this field (German Federal Statistical Office "Destatis" 2021; Just et al. 2017, p. 11).

The peculiarities of the real estate sector and real estate as a product make it impossible to simply adapt the general sustainability indicators developed in the existing literature without specific modifications. First, there are sector-specific stakeholders, e.g., investors, tenants, developers, employees, NGOs, banks, and the general public. As various stakeholders need real estate for different purposes, they each have different understandings of sustainability. Second, in the context of real estate investments, three assessment levels must be distinguished: the single asset, the fund, and the real estate company. At each level, the stakeholders might have divergent interests concerning sustainability (Bienert 2016, p. 32 ff.). In this article, we are focusing on the asset level. The third peculiarity is real estate's unique lifecycle, shown in Figure 1.

Figure 1

Real Estate Lifecycle

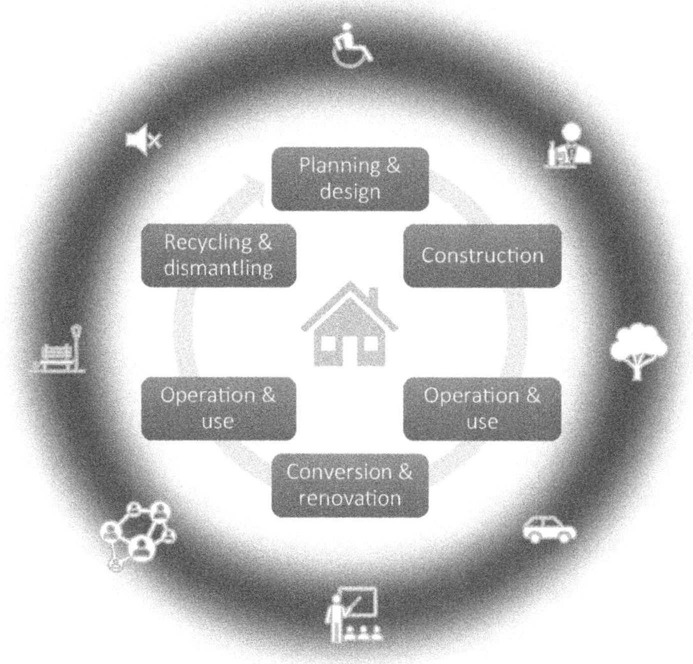

Source: Modified from Everling et al. 2009, p. 75.

On the one hand, the lifecycle is very long compared to other products. On the other hand, the lifecycle has specific stages like conversion followed by a second useful life and the eventual recycling and dismantling phase. Changes made during the renovation phase, which can affect sustainability during the second useful life, make it difficult to assess a real estate asset's sustainability for its entire lifecycle at the outset. Therefore, we suggest at the very least distinguishing between new, old and renovated real estate properties when comparing the real estate sustainability.

Compared to other long-lasting assets, real estate is a relatively expensive, inhomogeneous asset class that is only available to investors as a single property or in small numbers. The individual willingness of potential buyers to pay a price is hardly predictable, because many factors influence the price that go beyond the pure utility value, e. g., the location, the particular building style, the layout or the personal connection (Ghysels et al., p. 571).

3 Existing Research and Practical Approaches

The triple bottom line serves as the basic concept for our metric. This concept stems from socially responsible investing, which began in the 1960 s (Kleine 2009, p. 5). This investment strategy argues that financial success cannot be the only metric to measure success; there are non-financial factors without which companies and their projects cannot survive long term. Both Heins and Elkington claim to have invented the triple bottom line in the 1990 s (Kleine 2009, p. 5; Elkington 1998a, 1998b; Heins 1994). The triple bottom line divides non-financial factors, or rather sustainability, into three dimensions, i. e., pillars: E – environmental, S – social, and G – corporate governance. Nowadays, they are referred to as ESG factors. The development of the triple bottom line has given structure to the complex issue of sustainability (Kopfmüller et al. 2001; Kleine 2009, p. 5 ff.). The practice developed criteria and indicators to measure sustainability, based on the triple bottom line, but mainly focused on capital-oriented companies. With the development of sustainability indicators, the practice subdivides the three pillars into more granular subcategories aimed at assessing with as much detail and objectivity as possible (e. g., Refinitiv 2021, p. 3). This paper uses the term ESG indicators as a synonym for sustainability indicators.

Attempts to adapt these ESG indicators to real estate have various shortcomings (Walker et al. 2019, p. 19 ff.; Kleine 2009, p. 12 f.). Several certification guidelines developed by the practice exist, e. g., LEED (Leadership in Energy & Environmental Design) or DGNB (*Deutsche Gesellschaft für Nachhaltiges Bauen* "German Sustainable Building Council") as well as the organization GRESB (Global Real Estate Sustainability Benchmark) (Vieira de Castro et al. 2020, p. 253 ff.; Bienert 2016, p. 32 ff.). However, most certificates offered are limited to the environmental perspective and do not assess the social and corporate governance dimensions. Furthermore, the use of the certificates is criticized in the literature. They lead to unintended side effects because real estate is only built to meet the required standard but falls short of more extensive possibilities. As a result, sustainability is only superficially achieved. In addition, rating systems are often limited to specific regions, making it difficult to compare a larger number of real estate assets in different regions (Walker et al. 2019, p. 19 ff.; Kleine 2009, p. 12 f.).

From the addressees' perspective, certifications have two shortcomings. First, some only provide a binary evaluation: either the real estate is sustainable or not. However, the certificate is unlikely to meet the information requirements of all distinct investors or other stakeholders. Investors and other stakeholders are supposed to have further information interests. For instance, institutional investors (e. g., banks or insurance companies) require more detailed knowledge about each sustainability dimension's characteristics and target achievement levels, as well as the associated risks due to regulatory requirements (German Federal Financial Supervisory Authority "BaFin" 2020). At the same time, investors have a legitimate interest in knowing what deficiencies an existing, unsustainable real estate asset has. Second, other existing certifications are very detailed, require technical expertise, and are verbalized, making them impossible or time-consuming to comprehend without specialized knowledge. As a result, the assessments are not transparent from the stakeholder's point of view. Stakeholders are not enabled by existing certifications to form their own opinion on the sustainability of a real estate property.

Nevertheless, these certificates are used as indicators for real estate sustainability, too (Eichholtz et al. 2012, p. 1915), which shows that there is no differentiated metric as of yet. Additionally, Plößl and Just claim that data based on sustainability indicators are missing. Instead, they measure sustainability in real estate by using the growth rate of renewable energies to gross final energy consumption (Plößl and Just 2020, p. 23). In their analysis of existing approaches to assessing real estate sustainability Vieira de Castro et al. state that further research needs to be conducted to develop a holistic and detailed metric (Vieira de Castro et al. 2020, p. 267). The existing theoretical approaches often consider only one sustainability dimension like the Carbon Risk Real Estate Monitor (Spanner and Wein 2020) or the German Corporate Governance Code for the real estate sector (Institute for Corporate Governance in the German Real Estate Industry).

To the best of our knowledge, despite the vast amount of existing literature on single aspects of real estate sustainability, there is no holistic approach that applies the concept of the triple bottom line to real estate. Therefore, we aim to help fill this research gap by developing a concept in which the metric is based on sustainability indicators, using scores instead of a binary system that is compatible with standard databases.

4 **Concept**

4.1 From Sustainability Indicators to one ESG Score

In this section, we begin with describing our metric's system boundaries. We then explain the development of sustainability indicators in three steps. First, a literature review is conducted. Second, the adaptation of these indicators for real estate is examined. Third, real estate specific sustainability indicators from exposés and expert interviews are presented, which can complement the preexisting indicators. Following trends in recent literature, not only do we consider positive disclosed information, but controversies on sustainability issues, too (DasGupta 2021; Dorfleitner et al. 2020; Fiaschi et al. 2020; Nirino et al. 2021).

After developing sustainability indicators, we present our categorization idea and discuss the weighting of both categories and sustainability indicators, as shown in Figure 2.

Figure 2

Weighting of Sustainability Indicators and Categories

Source: Own illustration.

The observed sustainability indicators are then compiled in a checklist for investors to use. An example of a potential checklist is shown in Figure 3.

Figure 3

Sample Checklist

Sustainability indicator	Points	Indicator weight	Indicator score	Category	Sum of indicator scores	Category weight	Category score	Dimension	Dimension score	Total ESG score
Waste	1	0.12	0.12							
Water	1	0.14	0.14	Resources	0.26	0.15	0.04			
...	0	0.09	0.00							
Greenhouse gases	1	0.17	0.17							
Noise	0	0.09	0.00	Emissions	0.22	0.29	0.06	Environment	∑	∑
...	1	0.05	0.05							
		...	...							
...	...	...	...	...	∑	...	...			
		...	...							

Figure 3 *(Continued)*

Sustainability indicator	Points	Indicator weight	Indicator score	Category	Sum of indicator scores	Category weight	Category score	Dimension	Dimension score	Total ESG score
Work-life-balance	1	...	...							
On-the-job-safety	0	...	...	Working conditions	Σ	...	...			
...	0	...	...							
Donations	0	...	...							
Social housing	1	...	...	Corporate citizenship	Σ	...	...	Social	Σ	
...	1	...	...							
...	...	...	...							
...	...	...	...	Business ethics	Σ	...	...			
...	...	...	...							
Commercial offences	1	...	...							
Tax compliance	0	...	...	Compliance	Σ	...	...			
...	1	...	...							
...	...	...	...					Governance	Σ	
...	...	...	...	Risk	Σ	...	...			
...	...	...	...							
...	...	...	...							
...	...	...	...	...	Σ	...	...			
...	...	...	...							

Source: Own illustration.

To assess the sustainability of real estate the checklist user must read through the list and decide, whether there is positive, negative or no information about each indicator. If there is no or negative information regarding an indicator, we assign it zero points; we award one point if there is positive information. Each point is then multiplied with its specific indicator weight to calculate the sustainability indicator's score. These indicator scores are added up by category and multiplied with a specific category weight to calculate the overall category score. These category scores are combined to determine each dimension's score. Once dimension scores are added together, the total ESG score for a real estate asset is computed.[2]

4.2 System Boundaries

Before describing specifics on determining sustainability indicators, system boundaries must be defined for our concept.

2 Therefore, the calculation of the dimension scores and the overall ESG score is sectional linear. The sustainability indicators will be calculated in manifold ways.

As we are describing a concept for asset evaluation instead of performance measurement our spatial system boundary is broad. This means, that we do not only consider the asset but the surrounding area as well (see Figure 1). Here we must think in two directions: from inside the real estate property to the outsight and vice versa. To illustrate this for the environmental dimension, we can examine noise. On the one hand, noise, especially during construction, but also from people using the finished real estate property, affects animals and people in the surrounding area. On the other hand, noise from the outsight, e.g., passing trains, affects the people inside the real estate property. Moreover, considering both directions is socially meaningful. A family-friendly surrounding area that includes schools, playgrounds, and traffic-calmed zones affects real estate users (at least when considering residential buildings). In contrast, the real estate property socially affects the people in its surrounding area, because it shapes the landscape. To specify an explicit limitation of the surrounding area, we define it as a residential, industrial, or comparable area but not an entire city.

In terms of time, we consider the entire lifecycle at the asset level. To illustrate this, we can examine solar panels. Undoubtedly, using solar panels has a positive environmental impact. Nevertheless, disposing of these is problematic due to toxic components (Renner 2010, p. 553). Given this toxicity during the disposal period, we cannot simply focus on the years of use. The environmental impact of the entire lifecycle must be considered.

It is important to note that we do not consider the specific type of real estate tenant. For instance, we would not assess whether the tenant of, e.g., a shop sells tobacco or vegetables since such detail is subject to strong fluctuations and does not permanently change the real estate property itself.

4.3 Sustainability Indicators

The amount of information regarding sustainability disclosed by companies has rapidly increased during the last years (Chen et al. 2021, p. 152). As there is neither an exhaustive list of sustainability indicators nor mandatory sustainability indicators, hundreds of ESG indicators for investment products can be found in the literature and several databases. We conducted a literature review for our concept and compiled the sustainability indicators mentioned into a list (see Appendix). However, this list should only be viewed as a sample since it is not an exhaustive list of all sustainability indicators available in the literature. Most of the indicators have already been assigned to one of the three sustainability dimensions in the literature, since they were developed using the triple bottom line. For our table, we assigned the indicators to one of the three dimensions, if they had not previously been classified in the literature. This list is our starting point for developing sustainability indicators specifically for real estate.

After creating the lists, the sustainability indicators must be screened to select the ones useful in assessing real estate sustainability. The sustainability indicators that measure similar scopes are sorted together, e.g., "recovery/recycling" and "recycling" or "environmental policy" and "environmental policy/management". The next step is to exclude those sustainability indicators that are clearly non-applicable to real estate, e.g., "no revenues in tobacco" or "no revenues in weapons".

The sustainability indicators remaining after this screening are then adapted for real estate; adjustments are necessary due to the peculiarities of real estate. Water as a sustainability indicator perfectly illustrates why adjustments are needed. Looking at this from the perspective of a stock company's sneaker production, water would be an easy indicator to measure. To assess the water intensity for one pair of sneakers, it would be enough to determine, how much water is needed in the production plant, e. g., within one year and the number of sneakers produced within the same period. However, in the context of real estate, this is much more complex due to each real estate property's unique lifecycle and different assessment levels. Water is used in every lifecycle stage and by several parties. For instance, the company planning the real estate property and the construction company, e. g., for making the concrete. Once construction is completed, the real estate users' water consumption varies depending on their individual life-styles. Water use continues in the conversion and renovation stage and the second (or more) useful life (or lives), until the real estate property is finally dismantled.

Another aspect highlighting the need to adapt existing sustainability indicators for real estate is that some of the sustainability indicators may belong to multiple dimensions or blur between them, e. g., noise. To illustrate this, we continue with our sneakers example. When assessing the noise emission of sneakers, only the noise generated during production needs to be considered; noise produced during their useful life is irrelevant. Additionally, only noise stemming from sneaker production affects the environment; but obviously there is no effect the other way around. When assessing noise in the context of real estate, however, we have to consider the noise caused during construction that affects the environment, plus the noise generated inside the real estate property by daily use, e. g., a music school will produce a large volume of noise, not to mention further lifecycle stages. Additionally, the noise coming from outside the boundary into the real estate property, e. g., passing trains, must be taken into account – at this point, noise is not only an environmental indicator, but a social one, because people using the real estate are affected by it.

The examples of water consumption and noise show that sustainability indicators are more multifaceted, when adapted for the real estate and therefore need to be examined in a more differentiated manner that considers the whole lifecycle. Consequently, water consumption, noise, and other sustainability indicators must be measured separately for each lifecycle stage, considering different aspects like having state-of-the-art technical systems for water saving or sound protection.

So far, we have still only examined existing ESG indicators regularly used for standard investment products. After reviewing and selecting these sustainability indicators and adapting them for real estate on a theoretical basis, we proceed with real estate specific sustainability indicators that complement the existing ones. We begin by analyzing real estate based on exposés, prospectuses, remediation plans, and other informative documents. From such written descriptions, we can extract real estate specific sustainability indicators like family-friendliness, which can be measured by the number of schools or playgrounds in the surrounding area, accessibility through built-in stair lifts, or an eco-friendly infrastructure with public transportation.

Furthermore, we propose conducting expert interviews with architects, craftspeople, and engineers. Through these expert interviews, we anticipate learning about characteristics not expressly described in the analyzed documents, e. g., aspects that are standard from the author's point of view and therefore not mentioned or even negative aspects from an investor's point of view. For instance, if a rental house is to be sold, the exposé will not say that the bathroom is moldy despite this being relevant to a user's health. This is a valuable sustainability indicator in assessing the social dimension of sustainability.

Most sustainability indicators whose expressions can be derived from the analyzed documents, should be assigned to the environmental and social dimensions. This is because usually, only the finished asset itself is subject to an exposé, and no corporate governance-related information, e.g., the absence of undeclared work during the construction is disclosed. Therefore, to gather information about real estate specific corporate governance, we start by analyzing real estate companies' sustainability reports, including guidelines for dealing with industry-specific problems such as avoiding undeclared work among subcontractors. We then conduct further expert interviews. Useful experts could be investment company managers, construction company managers and employees, auditors and lawyers specializing in real estate cases, and real estate agents. In the interviews we would ask for internal guidelines, especially, e.g., regarding risk management, compliance, integrity, engagement and sustainability management, and recent court proceedings. Finally, to learn more about real estate specific controversies, public reporting from the last years is analyzed using qualitative content analysis.

The final step of developing sustainability indicators is validating their practicability. This step is needed to examine, which sustainability indicators are measurable and which are not suitable for practical use, e.g., due to a lack of information. This step begins with further analysis of exposés, prospectuses, remediation plans, and other informative documents, that had not been analyzed previously. We also propose conducting additional expert interviews. Moreover, we suggest analyzing publicly offered real estate, such as those presented on real estate portals. After the validation process, the sustainability indicators that are unmeasurable or unsuitable for practical use are excluded. This approach also allows other characteristics that we had not previously considered to be observed. In such cases, we would check whether to add these sustainability indicators and validate them iteratively.

4.4 Aggregation

As discussed in Section 4.3, many sustainability indicators become more complex in the context of real estate. Since absolute measures are impracticable for many sustainability indicators, we develop relative ones (cf. Bogenberger, p. 103 ff.). Using relative measures means that we compare the values of the sustainability indicators of interest for each real estate asset and divide them into five groups ranging from worst to best value.

To illustrate this, let us continue with our sneaker and water consumption example: If we wanted to assess the water intensity of a pair of sneakers, we could undoubtedly measure it in liters. Conversely, measuring a real estate property's water consumption for its entire lifecycle in absolute numbers is impossible at the outset. After all, there are too many unknowns in the future: we do not know how long the real estate property will be used and whether there will be periods of vacancy. Furthermore, we do not know, whether the real estate users will even try to conserve water. There are also significant regional differences in water use, as demonstrated in Figure 4. The variations in water consumption are not solely due to differences in technical standards; factors such as climate and cultural differences also play a role. Using such relative measures allows us to compare real estate sustainability despite regional differences. We rely on data from sources like public water and energy suppliers to develop these relative measures.

Figure 4

Total Freshwater Abstraction for Public Water Supply

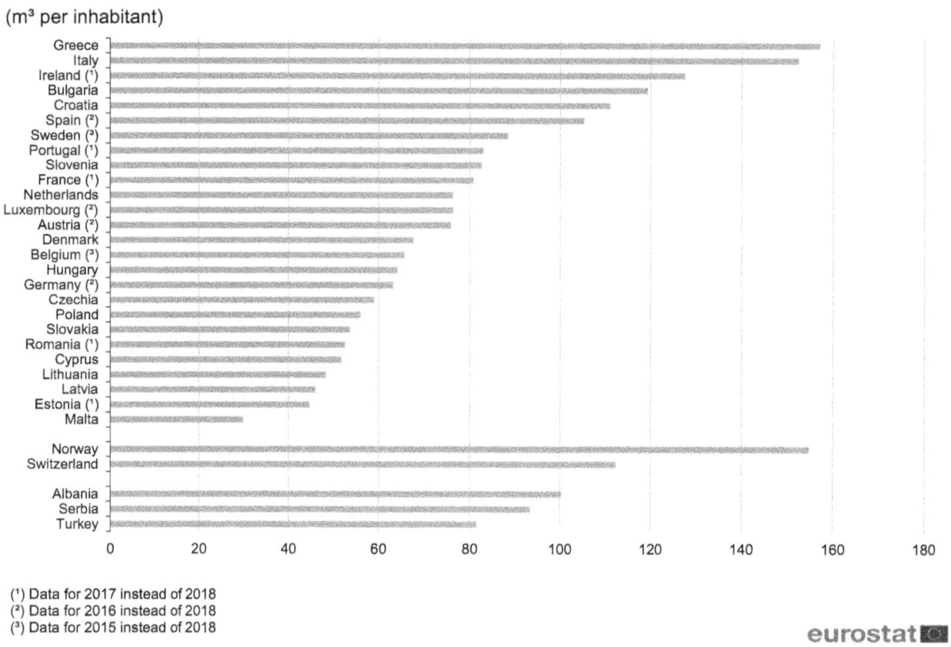

Source: Eurostat 2018.

The next aggregation step is to categorize the sustainability indicators. Since we already assigned each indicator to one of the sustainability dimensions during the literature review, we assign each sustainability indicator to a category. For instance, all diversity-related sustainability indicators could be grouped into one category, e. g., "nationalities on board", "women directors", and "board structure". A category named "pollutant emissions" could be created for sustainability indicators like "greenhouse gas emissions, scope 1", "greenhouse gas emissions, scope 2", "greenhouse gas emissions, scope 3", "NO_2 and SO_2 emissions", and "pollution control". The categorization results in a tree structure that begins with the sustainability indicators, e. g., "women directors", which interwine into categories, e. g., "diversity", before combining into dimensions and ending with the overall ESG score. The tree structure is illustrated in Figure 5. The tree structure will provide the users of our metric with a better overview of the sustainability indicators and allows the user of the metric to decide how many details they want to know.

Figure 5

Tree Structure of Sustainability Indicators, Categories, and Dimensions

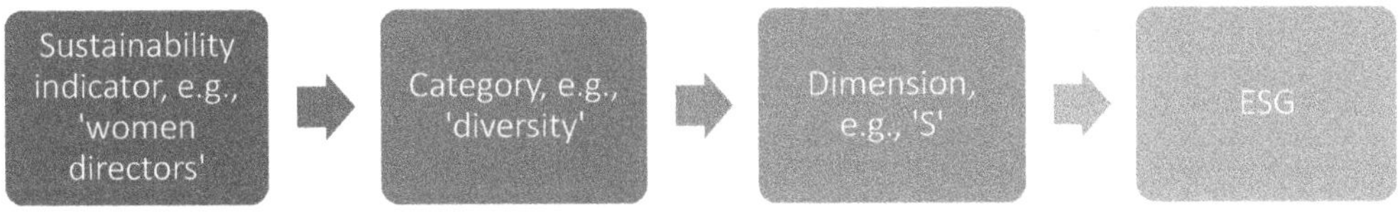

Source: Own illustration.

After the sustainability indicators and categories are defined, we gather them into a checklist. This checklist is only applicable at the asset level. Those who analyze a real estate asset can use the checklist to evaluate every sustainability indicator in a binary way, resulting in Boolean data. In other words, the answers are transferred into a system of zeros and ones. If a sustainability indicator applies, the value is one. If it does not apply or the information in question is unavailable, the value is zero. Since there are not only positive but also negative indicators, we define a polarity for each one. Therefore, the value determination is reversed for negative indicators, e.g., controversies on employee rights. If the user ticks yes, i.e., there have been recent controversies related to employee rights, the value is zero. If there are none, the value is one.

The categories are weighted differently. This is necessary for two reasons: First, if every reported detail is rewarded with one point the real estate asset that provides most information would automatically be classified as the most sustainable one. To prevent this, we propose to weight the categories depending on their materiality to assess real estate sustainability and the significance of their contribution toward reaching specific sustainability goals. Second, the weight scheme might stimulate transparency. Not providing highly material information leads to a worse result and cannot easily be compensated for with other, less material information (Refinitiv 2021, p. 3).

The regulations regarding sustainability disclosures do not explicitly influence how sustainability indicators are weighted for our metric. In contrast, our aim is to develop a metric that considers investors' understanding of sustainability, which can be congruent with current regulations or influenced by them, but not necessarily. From our point of view, there are two alternatives for weighting the categories: data-driven or stakeholder-driven. Databases commonly use data-driven weighting; for Boolean data, this is the transparency weights. When using this data-driven weighting, the level of disclosure is decisive for a category's weight. In other words, the categories most reported by companies are weighted as highly material and vice versa. A category's disclosure percentage is calculated to decide its weight. This percentage is determined by dividing the number of provided values for a category by the number of relevant reporting companies. These disclosure percentages are then converted into decile ranks, i.e., from 1 to 10 (Refinitiv 2021, 10 ff.).

An alternative to the data-driven approach is weighting by stakeholder surveys. We assume that stakeholder groups, such as users, investors, architects and financiers, have different understandings of sustainability. To find out what sustainability means from the investors' perspectives, we propose conducting a survey among them. From this survey, we can derive one uppermost goal for each dimension, e.g., climate protection for the environmental dimension, health for the social dimension, or going concern for corporate governance. Depending on their contribution to the uppermost goal, we would assign a weight between 1 and 10 to determine each category's score. If a category is important for attaining a dimension's uppermost goal, it is given a weight of 10. If it is less important, the weight is progressively reduced by 1. For instance, if we find out that the existence of a combined heat and power plant is significant in reaching the uppermost environmental goal of reducing carbon emissions, we would assign 1 point if such an installation exists and multiply it by the weight of 10. The default weight is 5.

An advantage of data-driven weighting is that it is objective and impartial; it only depends on the information provided. Additionally, it is flexible and continually adjusts itself to the current reporting practice. In comparison, stakeholder-driven weighting is fixed: investor surveys must be conducted repeatedly to adjust the weightings. Thus, the stakeholder-driven weighting is inflexible and time intensive, while the data-driven one works automatically. Although it is time intensive, a great advantage of the stakeholder-driven weighting is that the investors' understanding of sustainability is reflected. Data-driven weighting does not allow for different weightings and therefore, different understandings of sustainability between stakeholder groups. Since it depends on the data provided by companies, or rather real estate owners, the data-driven weighting only considers a single stakeholder's understanding of sustainability, i.e. the understanding of reporting companies. It is also possible that in data-driven weighting, easy-to-generate data are disclosed instead of the data actually material to reaching sustainability goals. A disadvantage of the stakeholder-driven weighting is that it could lead to results without extremes. If one investor classifies a sustainability indicator as rather immaterial another as highly material, the result is that it is moderately material. The results from data-driven weighting are clearer since they show the extremes.

In conclusion, both approaches to weighting the categories have their merits. From our perspective, stakeholder-driven weighting is preferable because it considers the needs and attitudes of each stakeholder group as summarized in Figure 2. However, since the data-driven weighting is not as time intensive, we suggest to use this approach additionally and compare the results afterward. In both cases, the weights are normalized into percentages.

The sustainability indicators have to be weighted within the categories, too, before ultimately being normalized into percentages. The sustainability indicators' weights depend on their contribution to a category's specific assigned goal. For some sustainability indicators, evaluating their contribution to the category goal might be straightforward, e.g., carbon emissions can be quantified. Expert interviews with engineers should be conducted for sustainability indicators within the environmental dimension. Estimating the importance of sustainability indicators within social and corporate governance dimensions might prove more difficult. For some social indicators, expert interviews with doctors, psychologists, and city planners could be helpful. Additionally, we propose conducting a survey among real estate users on what makes them feel comfortable in a real estate property. Interviews should be done with auditors, consultants, lawyers and managers to discover what is most important in the corporate governance dimension.

4.5 Ranking

Before the sustainability of real estate assets can be compared, the assets need to be clustered, because some sustainability indicators and weights vary depending on the real estate use type. For instance, in the COVID-19 crisis, air filtration might be more important in public real estate, e.g., schools, than in private houses. Furthermore, following the literature, we must distinguish real estate assets by their current lifecycle stage (Buyle et al. 2013; Vladimirova et al. 2018; Sharma et al.

2011; Ristimäki et al. 2013; König and Cristofaro 2012). After all, nearly every new real estate project will appear sustainable compared to an old one, regardless of whether it is truly that sustainable, i.e., when compared to other projects in the same lifecycle stage. Therefore, to ensure that only similar real estate assets are compared, they must be clustered into a grid that differentiates by use type and lifecycle stage. At a minimum, the use types should be separated into private, commercial and public. The lifecycle stage should be differentiated as new, renovated, or old at the very least. Figure 6 displays the planned real estate clustering.

Figure 6

Cluster Grid for Real Estate Properties

		Lifecycle stage		
Use type		New	Renovated	Old
	Private			
	Commercial			
	Public			

Source: Own illustration.

In addition to the distinctions shown in Figure 6, the practice could add further distinctions, e.g., the reason for the assessment. We assume that an assessment's purpose affects its result. For instance, if a bank plans to build new apartment buildings and attempts to acquire investors, the sustainability of the real estate assets is mainly assessed based on exposés. Both circumstances contribute to a relatively high sustainability score because the real estate project is presented in the best light when trying to acquire investors and more generally, when discussed in exposés. In contrast, if the agency responsible for a public real estate property applies for money to remediate its real estate property, the agency would emphasize the property's weaknesses.

After the clusters are determined, real estate within the same cluster can be compared using their ESG score. This comparison could be made by either absolute or relative thresholds. Although relative thresholds suffer from the disadvantage that the best are not necessarily good, this approach has several advantages. First, the evaluation changes over time automatically. When the sustainability of one real estate asset is strengthened, it improves or rather becomes more sustainable relative to other properties. Second, there may be sustainability indicators where data are completely unavailable. In such cases it should not negatively impact on the ESG score. Relative thresholds, are flexible and avoid unattainable goals. Third, when using relative thresholds, we do not have to decide which score is enough to be sustainable. This is precisely the issue with certificates, where simply exceeding a threshold makes real estate sustainable, and details are no longer important. Due to these advantages, we have decided in favor of relative thresholds, i.e., percentiles. Following established databases, we calculate the percentile rank score as follows (Dorfleitner et al. 2020, p. 397; Ronald Rousseau 2012, p. 417):

$$\text{percentile rank score} = \frac{\text{no. of companies with a worse value} + \frac{\text{no. of companies with the same value including the current one}}{2}}{\text{no. of companies with a value}}$$

The resulting percentile rank scores could be classified, e. g., from A … to D …, where A … represents the best ESG performance and the highest level of transparency and D … the worst. The exact classification and thresholds depend on subsequent validation.

4.6 Validation of the Metric

At this point, the sustainability indicators have been validated, but their aggregation, weighting, and the ranking have not. The empirical validation of the aggregation, weighting, and ranking is essential to ensure that

1. assessing the sustainability of two or more real estate assets with the same sustainability characteristics leads to identical ESG scores when using our metric;
2. assessing real estate assets with our metric leads to a coherent overall evaluation;
3. ranking real estate assets based on our metric's assessment is comprehensible and corresponds to human perception;
4. valuating also works out-of-sample, i. e., when applied to real estate assets not part of the previous analyses conducted during the metric's development.

For these purposes, additional material on real estate must be collected and analyzed on a larger scale.

5 **Conclusion**

This paper aimed to present our idea of a concept for a real estate sustainability metric and real estate specific indicators at the asset level. Although there is an increasing demand for sustainable investment products, including real estate, investors suffer from a lack of information regarding the offered products. Moreover, increasing regulations are a driving factor in the need for sustainability indicators.

Although several ESG indicators are found in the literature and various databases, they cannot be used without adjustments due to the peculiarities of real estate, i. e., sector-specific stakeholders, the three assessment levels and the unique lifecycle of real estate properties. Due to these peculiarities, a real estate specific metric for sustainability and sustainability indicators are necessary. Different theoretical and practical approaches to assessing real estate sustainability exist, but these either focused on only one of the three sustainability dimensions or offered a binary evaluation, i. e., "sustainable" or "not sustainable".

For our metric, the triple bottom line served as the basic concept. Developing real estate specific sustainability indicators begins with a literature review to extract the relevant sustainability indicators. These relevant indicators are adapted for real estate and then complemented by real estate specific sustainability indicators. The developed sustainability indicators then have to be weighted based on expert interviews and assigned to categories. As discussed in Section 4.4, the categories could be weighted with either a data-driven or stakeholder-driven approach. We decided on the latter.

These categories, consisting of several sustainability indicators, are assigned to the ESG dimensions. All three levels of our metric are summarized in a checklist. To assess real estate sustainability, the checklist users must work through the list and decide, whether there is positive, negative, or no information for each sustainability indicator. Based on the weighted results for each sustainability indicator, the category scores are calculated and combined to determine a dimension score and, ultimately, an ESG score. The ESG scores are then compared based on the percentile rank score.

Our contribution to the literature is the idea of how to develop a concept that provides a transparent and holistic assessment of real estate sustainability. Moreover, our checklist is less complicated than certifications and requires neither expert knowledge nor much time.

The concept of the metric as presented in this paper is limited to the investors' perspective. Further research should be conducted to extend the metric to help even more stakeholder groups, e. g., users. Additionally, the metric is limited to sustainability assessment of assets. Further research must be conducted on aggregating the ESG scores at the asset level to determine an ESG score at the fund or company level. Based on our metric, gap analyses could be conducted with minor modifications, too. Furthermore, our metric could be extended to a concept for real estate sustainability risk assessments that banks and fund managers need.

References

— Alda, Mercedes (2021): The environmental, social, and governance (ESG) dimension of firms in which social responsible investment (SRI) and conventional pension funds invest: The mainstream SRI and the ESG inclusion. *Journal of Cleaner Production* 298 (2), p. 126812. DOI: 10.1016/j.jclepro.2021.126812.

— Baier, Philipp, Marc Berninger, and Florian Kiesel (2020): Environmental, social and governance reporting in annual reports: A textual analysis. *Financial Markets, Institutions & Instruments* 29 (3), pp. 93–118. DOI: 10.1111/fmii.12132.

— Bassen, Alexander and Ana Maria Kovács (2020): Environmental, Social and Governance Key Performance Indicators from a Capital Market Perspective. In: Thomas Beschorner, Alexander Brink, Bettina Hollstein, Marc C. Hübscher, Olaf Schumann (Eds.): Wirtschafts- und Unternehmensethik. Wiesbaden: Springer Fachmedien Wiesbaden, pp. 809–820, checked on 11/27/2021.

— Bausch, Olaf and Thomas Voller (Eds.) (2020): Geldwäsche-Compliance. Wiesbaden: Springer Fachmedien Wiesbaden.

— Berg, Florian, Julian F. Koelbel, and Roberto Rigobon (2019): Aggregate Confusion: The Divergence of ESG Ratings. Available online at https://ssrn.com/abstract=3438533, checked on 11/29/2021.

— Beschorner, Thomas, Alexander Brink, Bettina Hollstein, Marc C. Hübscher, and Olaf Schumann (Eds.) (2020): Wirtschafts- und Unternehmensethik. Wiesbaden: Springer Fachmedien Wiesbaden.

— Bienert, Sven (2016): Metastudie: Nachhaltigkeit contra Rendite? Die Implikationen nachhaltigen Wirtschaftens für offene Immobilienfonds am Beispiel der Deka Immobilien Investment GmbH und der WestInvest GmbH. *IRE|BS, Beiträge zur Immobilienwirtschaft* (14).

— Bogenberger, Stefan: Entwicklung eines Immobilien-Benchmarkings. In: Immobilien-Benchmarking, pp. 89–120, checked on 11/29/2021.

— Buyle, Matthias, Johan Braet, and Amaryllis Audenaert (2013): Life cycle assessment in the construction sector: A review. *Renewable and Sustainable Energy Reviews* 26, pp. 379–388. DOI: 10.1016/j.rser.2013.05.001.
— BVI (2021): Investmentstatistik, checked on 11/18/2021.
— Chatterji, Aaron K., David I. Levine, and Michael W. Toffel, (2009): How Well Do Social Ratings Actually Measure Corporate Social Responsibility? *Journal of Economics & Management* 18 (1), pp. 125–169.
— Chen, Mike, Robert von Behren, and George Mussalli (2021): The Unreasonable Attractiveness of More ESG Data. *The Journal of Portfolio Management* 48 (1), pp. 147–162. DOI: 10.3905/jpm.2021.1.281.
— Consumer Advice Centre "Verbraucherzentrale" (2021): Geld nachhaltig anlegen – wie Sie vorgehen können und was schwierig ist | Verbraucherzentrale.de. Available online at https://www.verbraucherzentrale.de/wissen/geld-versicherungen/nachhaltige-geldanlage/geld-nachhaltig-anlegen-wie-sie-vorgehen-koennen-und-was-schwierig-ist-11071, updated on 2021, checked on 11/20/2021.
— DasGupta, Ranjan (2021): Financial performance shortfall, ESG controversies, and ESG performance: Evidence from firms around the world. *Finance Research Letters*, p. 102487. DOI: 10.1016/j.frl.2021.102487.
— Daugaard, Dan (2020): Emerging new themes in environmental, social and governance investing: a systematic literature review. *Accounting & Finance* 60 (2), pp. 1501–1530. DOI: 10.1111/acfi.12479.
— Dorfleitner, Gregor, Christian Kreuzer, and Christian Sparrer (2020): ESG controversies and controversial ESG: about silent saints and small sinners. *Journal of Asset Management* 21 (5), pp. 393–412. DOI: 10.1057/s41260-020-00178-x.
— Drempetic, Samuel, Christian Klein, and Bernhard Zwergel (2020): The Influence of Firm Size on the ESG Score: Corporate Sustainability Ratings Under Review. *Journal of Business Ethics* 167 (2), pp. 333–360. DOI: 10.1007/s10551-019-04164–1.
— DVFA (2008): KPI for ESG Sektoren edited. Available online at https://www.dvfa.de/fileadmin/downloads/Publikationen/Standards/KPIs_for_ESG_3_0_Final.pdf, checked on 11/27/2021.
— Eichholtz, Piet, Nils Kok, and Erkan Yonder (2012): Portfolio greenness and the financial performance of REITs. *Journal of International Money and Finance* 31 (7), pp. 1911–1929. DOI: 10.1016/j.jimonfin.2012.05.014.
— Elkington, John (1998a): Accounting for the Triple Bottom Line. *Measuring Business Excellence* 2 (3), pp. 18–22. DOI: 10.1108/eb025539.
— Elkington, John (1998b): Partnerships from cannibals with forks: The triple bottom line of 21st-century business. *Environmental Quality Management*, pp. 37–51.
— European Commission (2019): The EU Sustainability Taxonomy: a Financial Impact Assessment. JRC Technical Reports.
— European Labour Authority (2021): The European Platform tackling undeclared work. Available online at https://www.ela.europa.eu/en/european-platform-tackling-undeclared-work, checked on 11/29/2021.
— European Union (2018): Directive (EU) 2018/ of the European Parliament and of the Council of 30 May 2018 amending Directive (EU) 2015/849 on the prevention of the use of the financial system for the purposes of money laundering or terrorist financing, and amending Directives 2009/138/EC and 2013/36/EU. Available online at https://eur-lex.europa.eu/legal-content/EN/TXT/?uri=celex%3A32018L0851, checked on 11/29/2021.

- European Union (2019): Regulation (EU) 2019/2088 of the European Parliament and of the Council of 27 November 2019 on sustainability-related disclosures in the financial services sector. SFDR. Available online at https://eur-lex.europa.eu/eli/reg/2019/2088/oj, checked on 11/18/2021.
- Eurostat (2018): Total freshwater abstraction for public water supply. Available online at https://ec.europa.eu/eurostat/statistics-explained/index.php?title=File:Total_freshwater_abstraction_for_public_water_supply,_2018_(m%C2%B3_per_inhabitant).png#filelinks, checked on 11/28/2021.
- Everling, Oliver, Olaf Jahn, and Elisabeth Kammermeier (2009): Rating von Einzelhandelsimmobilien. Qualität, Potenziale und Risiken sicher bewerten. 1. Aufl. Wiesbaden: Gabler Verlag/GWV Fachverlage GmbH Wiesbaden. Available online at http://gbv.eblib.com/patron/FullRecord.aspx?p=748438.
- EY (2021): Nachhaltigkeit: Immobilienfondsmanager hinken eigenen Ansprüchen hinterher, 2021. Available online at https://www.ey.com/de_de/news/2021/03/ey-snapshot-2021, checked on 6/15/2021.
- Fiaschi, Davide, Elisa Giuliani, Federica Nieri, and Nicola Salvati (2020): How bad is your company? Measuring corporate wrongdoing beyond the magic of ESG metrics. *Business Horizons* 63 (3), pp. 287–299. DOI: 10.1016/j.bushor.2019.09.004.
- FNG (2021): Marktbericht Nachhaltige Geldanlagen 2021. Available online at https://www.forum-ng.org/fileadmin/Marktbericht/2021/FNG_Marktbericht2021_Online.pdf.
- Fowler, Stephen J. and C. Hope (2007): A Critical Review of Sustainable Business Indices and their Impact. *J Bus Ethics* 76 (3), pp. 243–252. DOI: 10.1007/s10551-007-9590–2.
- German Federal Criminal Police Office (2012): Fachstudie "Geldwäsche im Immobiliensektor in Deutschland" – Managementfassung. Available online at https://www.bka.de/SharedDocs/Downloads/DE/UnsereAufgaben/Deliktsbereiche/GeldwaescheFIU/fiuFachstudieGeldwaescheImmobiliensektor.html.
- German Federal Environmental Agency "Umweltbundesamt" (2021): "Grüne" Produkte: Marktzahlen. Available online at https://www.umweltbundesamt.de/daten/private-haushalte-konsum/konsum-produkte/gruene-produkte-marktzahlen#umsatz-mit-grunen-produkten, updated on 4/21/2021, checked on 4/21/2021.
- German Federal Financial Supervisory Authority "BaFin" (2020): Merkblatt zum Umgang mit Nachhaltigkeitsrisiken. Available online at https://www.bafin.de/SharedDocs/Downloads/DE/Merkblatt/dl_mb_Nachhaltigkeitsrisiken.pdf?__blob=publicationFile&v=9, checked on 2/16/2021.
- German Federal Government (2020): Grundlage für CO2-Preis steht. Available online at https://www.bundesregierung.de/breg-de/themen/klimaschutz/nationaler-emissionshandel-1684508, checked on 2/12/2021.
- German Federal Ministry of Finance "Bundesfinanzministerium" (2020): Gesetz zur Umsetzung der Änderungsrichtlinie zur Vierten EU-Geldwäscherichtlinie – Bundesfinanzministerium – Service. Available online at https://www.bundesfinanzministerium.de/Content/DE/Gesetzestexte/Gesetze_Gesetzesvorhaben/Abteilungen/Abteilung_VII/19_Legislaturperiode/2019-12-19-Gesetz-4-EU-Geldwaescherichtlinie/0-Gesetz.html, checked on 11/29/2021.
- German Federal Ministry of Finance "Bundesfinanzministerium" (2021): Gesetz zur europäischen Vernetzung der Transparenzregister und zur Umsetzung der Richtlinie (EU) 2019/1153 des Europäischen Parlaments und des Rates vom 20. Juni 2019 zur Nutzung von Finanzinformationen für die Bekämpfung von Geldwäsche, Terrorismusfinanzierung und sonstigen schweren Straftaten (Transparenzregister- und Finanzinformationsgesetz) – Bundesfinanzministerium – Service. Available online at https://www.bundesfinanzministerium.

de/Content/DE/Gesetzestexte/Gesetze_Gesetzesvorhaben/Abteilungen/Abteilung_VII/19_Legislaturperiode/2021-06-30-TraFinG/0-Gesetz.html, checked on 11/29/2021.
— German Federal Statistical Office "Destatis" (2021): Beschäftigte, Umsatz im Bauhauptgewerbe (Messzahlen und Veränderungsraten): Deutschland, Monate, Wirtschaftszweige. Available online at https://www-genesis.destatis.de/genesis/online?sequenz=tabelleErgebnis&selectionname=44151-0001&leerzeilen=false&zeitscheiben=3#abreadcrumb, checked on 2/16/2021.
— Ghysels, Eric, Alberto Plazzi, Rossen Valkanov, and Walter Torous: Forecasting Real Estate Prices. *Handbook of Economic Forecasting* 2, pp. 509–580.
— Hahn, Rüdiger and Michael Kühnen (2013): Determinants of sustainability reporting: a review of results, trends, theory, and opportunities in an expanding field of research. *Journal of Cleaner Production* 59, pp. 5–21. DOI: 10.1016/j.jclepro.2013.07.005.
— Heins, Bernd (1994): Nachhaltige Entwicklung – aus sozialer Sicht. *Zeitschrift für angewandte Umweltforschung* 7 (1–4), pp. 19–25.
— Institute for Corporate Governance in the German Real Estate Industry: Corporate Governance Code of the German Real Estate Industry 2020. Available online at https://www.icg-institut.de/wp-content/uploads/2020/09/AG-Kodex-neu-2017-2.pdf.
— Just, Tobias, Michael Voigtländer, Rupert Eisfeld, Ralph Henger, Markus Hesse, and Alexandra Troschka (2017): Wirtschaftsfaktor Immobilien 2017. Edited by Deutscher Verband für Wohnungswesen, Städtebau und Raumordnung e. V. Available online at https://www.iwkoeln.de/fileadmin/publikationen/2017/345334/Gutachten_Wirtschaftsfaktor-Immobilien_2017_6.pdf, checked on 2/17/2021.
— Kleine, Alexandro (2009): Operationalisierung einer Nachhaltigkeitsstrategie. Ökologie, Ökonomie und Soziales integrieren. @Kaiserslautern, Techn. Univ., Diss. 2008. 1. Aufl. Wiesbaden: Gabler Verlag/GWV Fachverlage GmbH Wiesbaden (Gabler Edition Wissenschaft). Available online at http://dx.doi.org/10.1007/978-3-8349-9414-1.
— König, Holger and M. Lisa de Cristofaro (2012): Benchmarks for life cycle costs and life cycle assessment of residential buildings. *Building Research & Information* 40 (5), pp. 558–580. DOI: 10.1080/09613218.2012.702017.
— Kopfmüller, Jürgen, Volker Brandl, Juliane Jörissen, Michael Paetau, Gerhard Banse, Reinhard Coenen, and Armin Grunwald (2001): Nachhaltige Entwicklung integrativ betrachtet. Konstitutive Elemente, Regeln, Indikatoren. Berlin: edition sigma (1).
— Nirino, Niccolò, Gabriele Santoro, Nicola Miglietta, and Roberto Quaglia (2021): Corporate controversies and company's financial performance: Exploring the moderating role of ESG practices. *Technological Forecasting and Social Change* 162, p. 120341. DOI: 10.1016/j.techfore.2020.120341.
— O'Rourke, Anastasia (2003): The message and methods of ethical investment. *Journal of Cleaner Production* 11 (6), pp. 683–693. DOI: 10.1016/S0959-6526(02)00105-1.
— Park, So Ra and Jae Young Jang (2021): The Impact of ESG Management on Investment Decision: Institutional Investors' Perceptions of Country-Specific ESG Criteria. *International Journal of Financial Studies* 9 (3), p. 48. DOI: 10.3390/ijfs9030048.
— Plößl, Franziska and Tobias Just (2020): Megatrends in der Immobilienwirtschaft. Textbasierte Trend- und Stimmungsanalyse. *IRE|BS, Beiträge zur Immobilienwirtschaft* (24).
— PwC and the Urban Land Institute (2020): Emerging Trends in Real Estate. Europe 2020. Available online at www.pwc.com/emerging-trends-real-estate/europe-202, checked on 2/14/2021.

- Refinitiv (2021): Environmental, Social and Governance (ESG) Scores from Refinitiv. Available online at https://www.refinitiv.com/content/dam/marketing/en_us/documents/methodology/refinitiv-esg-scores-methodology.pdf#page=3&zoom=auto,-850,350.
- Renner, Oliver (2010): Grundlagen der Solarenergie. In Matthias Kramer (Ed.): Integratives Umweltmanagement. Wiesbaden: Gabler, pp. 553–561.
- Ristimäki, Miro, Antti Säynäjoki, Jukka Heinonen, and Seppo Junnila (2013): Combining life cycle costing and life cycle assessment for an analysis of a new residential district energy system design. *Energy* 63 (1), pp. 168–179. DOI: 10.1016/j.energy.2013.10.030.
- Rogmans, Tim and Mohammad Ghunaim (2016): A framework for evaluating sustainability indicators in the real estate industry. *Ecological Indicators* 66 (2001), pp. 603–611. DOI: 10.1016/j.ecolind.2016.01.058.
- Rousseau, Ronald (2012): Basic properties of both percentile rank scores and the I3 indicator. *Journal of the American Society for Information Science and Technology* 63 (2), pp. 416–420. DOI: 10.1002/asi.21684.
- Schultze, Wolfgang and Ramona Trommer (2012): The concept of environmental performance and its measurement in empirical studies. *J Manag Control* 22 (4), pp. 375–412. DOI: 10.1007/s00187-011-0146-3.
- Sharma, Aashish, Abhishek Saxena, Muneesh Sethi, Venu Shree, Varun Goel (2011): Life cycle assessment of buildings: A review. *Renewable and Sustainable Energy Reviews* 15 (1), pp. 871–875. DOI: 10.1016/j.rser.2010.09.008.
- Spanner, Maximilian M. and Julia Wein (2020): Carbon risk real estate monitor: making decarbonisation in the real estate sector measurable. *JERER* 13 (3), pp. 277–299. DOI: 10.1108/JERER-05-2020-0031.
- Vieira de Castro, Aliane, Gema Ramírez Pacheco, and Fco. Javier Neila González (2020): Holistic Approach to the sustainable commercial property business. Analysis of the main Existing sustainable certifications. *International Journal of Strategic Property Management* 24 (4), pp. 251–268. DOI: 10.3846/ijspm.2020.12174.
- Vladimirova, Irina, Galina Kallaur, and Kseniia Bareshenkova (2018): Digital methods of real estate asset lifecycle management. *Baltic Journal of Real Estate Economics and Construction Management* 6 (1), pp. 165–174. DOI: 10.2478/bjreecm-2018-0013.
- Walker, Thomas, Cary Krosinsky, Lisa N. Hasan, and Stéfanie D. Kibsey (2019): Sustainable Real Estate. Multidisciplinary Approaches to an Evolving System. Cham, Schweiz: Palgrave Macmillan.

Appendix

Table 1

Environmental	Social	Corporate Governance
Access to land	Absenteeism	Anti-competitive behavior, monopoly
Agricultural chemicals	Access to basic services	Anti-competitive practices
Alternative fuels	Access to healthcare	Audit
Animal Welfare	Access to medicine	Audit and control
Announcement of environmental awards	Charity	Board
Beneficial products and services	Child labor	Board diversity
Biodiversity	Clinical trials	Board structure

Table 1 *(Continued)*

Environmental	Social	Corporate Governance
Biodiversity management	Collective bargaining	Bribery and corruption
Biofuels	Community relations	Business ethics
Certification status	Community and society	
Chemical controls	Corporate citizenship/philanthropy	CEO reputation
Chemical or oil spills	Customer relationship	Chair/CEO role
Climate change	Customer satisfaction	Chairperson-CEO separation
Climate change strategy	Diversity	Climate risk management
CO_2 emissions	Education	Codes of conduct
Competence and commitment and policy and goals	Employee development	Committees
Deployment of renewable energy sources	Employee turnover	Compensation of directors[3]
Eco-product/process strategy	Employment	Compliance
Ecosystem service	External social policy	Contributions to political parties
Electromagnetic fields	Health and safety	Corporate governance
Emissions	Health and safety of products	Corruption
Emissions management and reporting	HIV and AIDS	Customer relationship management
End-of-lifecycle impact	HIV programs	Dimension of pending legal proceedings
Energy	Human capital development	Disclosure and reporting
Energy efficiency	Human resources management	Employee representatives
Environmental brochures	Human rights	ESG incentives
Environmental compatibility	ILO core conventions	Ethical behavior
Environmental compatibility of products	Indigenous rights	Ethical economic policy
Environmental evaluation or conditions placed on suppliers	Internal social policy	Extent of stakeholder dialogue
Environmental fines	Knowledge management	Financial inclusion
Environmental impact of the product(s)	Labor practice indicators	Financial robustness
Environmental index based on SO_2, NO_x and COD emissions per production unit	Labor practices	Formal governance policy
Environmental liabilities	Labor standards	Global compact membership
Environmental management	Maturity of workforce	Governance of sustainability issues
Environmental management system	No revenues in alcohol	Independent directors
Environmental performance	No revenues in gambling	Investor relations
Environmental policy	No revenues in gaming	Law suits, fines and penalties
Environmental policy/management	No revenues in nuclear power	Litigation payments
Environmental reporting	No revenues in tobacco	Lobbying
Environmental standards	No revenues in uranium	Management
Environmentally-driven commercial development	No revenues in weapons	Management consulting/auditors
Forests	Nutrition	Nationalities on board

3 There are several indicators that blur between the dimensions. E.g., "remuneration" and "compensation of directors" could be classified as social or corporate governance-related indicator. In this table, we decided to follow the literature and classified "remuneration" as social and "compensation of directors" as corporate governance-related indicator. This classification seems reasonable, because "remuneration" is rather the salary of the employees and influences their wealth, while "compensation of directors" touches the management structure, e.g., by incentives.

Table 1 *(Continued)*

Environmental	Social	Corporate Governance
GHG emissions	Partnership with subcontractor	Number of board members
GHG policies	Privacy and free expression	Political influence
GMOs	Product safety	Privacy and IT
Green buildings	Public health	Regulatory problems
Green products	Remuneration	Renumeration
Greenhouse gas emissions, scope 1	Restructuring-related relocation of jobs	Reporting quality
Greenhouse gas emissions, scope 2	Security	Responsible marketing
Greenhouse gas emissions, scope 3	Site closure	Risk & crisis management
Hazardous waste	Social and political contribution	Risk & opportunities management
Innovation	Social reporting	Scorecards/measurement systems
Low Carbon	Society	Shareholders
Material and energy consumption	Staff turnover	Shareholder rights
Nature loss	Stakeholder Engagement	Stakeholder engagement
News on environmental investments	Standards for suppliers	Strategic planning
Non-GHG air emissions	Supply chain	Sustainability management and reporting
NO_2 and SO_2 emissions	Supply chain labor standards	Sustainability relations with stakeholders
Organization of the environmental program	Talent attraction & retention	Sustainable finance
Ozone-depleting chemicals	Training & qualification	Systemic risk
Ozone-depleting gases	Unions	Taxes
Packages	Weak governance zones	Transparency
Permit denials or shut-ins	Workforce	UNGC compliance
Pollution control		Whistle-blowing system
Pollution prevention		Women directors
Pounds of toxic chemical emissions		
Product development		
Product opportunities		
Quality of environmental and annual report		
Ratio of toxic waste recycled to total toxic waste generated		
Recovery/recycling		
Recycling		
Regulatory penalty value		
Renewable energy sources		
Resource depletion		
Resource efficiency		
Resource use		
Role of the executive in environmental work		
Substantial emissions		
Supply chain environmental standards		
Toxic spills		
Transportation		
Types of raw materials used		

Table 1 *(Continued)*

Environmental	Social	Corporate Governance
Use of audits		
use of eco-labels		
Waste		
Waste and recycling		
Water		

Compilation of ESG Indicators from the Literature (Alda 2021; Baier et al. 2020; Bassen and Kovács 2020; Beschorner et al. 2020; Chatterji, Aaron K., Levine, David I. and Toffel 2009; Daugaard 2020; Drempetic et al. 2020; DVFA 2008; Fowler and Hope 2007; Hahn and Kühnen 2013; O'Rourke 2003; Park and Jang 2021; Schultze and Trommer 2012; Dorfleitner et al. 2020; Berg et al. 2019).

Sustainable Financial Literacy and Preferences for Sustainable Investments among Young Adults

ARMIN VARMAZ, KATHARINA RIEBE AND SABRINA HEGNER

Armin Varmaz, School of International Business Bremen, e-mail: armin.varmaz@hs-bremen.de
Katharina Riebe, City University of Applied Sciences Bremen, e-mail: katharina.riebe@hs-bremen.de
Sabrina Hegner, School of International Business Bremen, e-mail: sabrina.hegner@hs-bremen.de

Abstract: We use a choice experiment on equity fund investments to estimate the preferences of young adults for sustainable investments relative to conventional investment funds. Our results suggest that the traditional trade-off between investment fund risk and return is still valid in the selection of sustainable investment funds. The environment focus is more important for the choice of sustainable investment then social or governance aspects. Latent behavioural characteristics (conscientiousness, importance of the impact of direct investments on sustainability, risk aversion, financial literacy) are also important to explain the choice for sustainable funds.

Zusammenfassung: In diesem Beitrag verwenden wir ein Auswahlexperiment bzgl. der Auswahl von Aktienfonds, um die Präferenzen junger Erwachsener für nachhaltige Anlagen im Vergleich zu konventionellen Investmentfonds zu schätzen. Unsere Ergebnisse deuten darauf hin, dass der traditionelle Trade-Off zwischen dem Risiko und der Rendite von Aktienfonds auch bei der Auswahl nachhaltiger Investmentfonds Bestand hat. Der Fokus auf die Umwelt ist bei der Wahl nachhaltiger Anlagen wichtiger als soziale oder Governance-Aspekte. Latente Verhaltensmerkmale (Gewissenhaftigkeit, Bedeutung der Auswirkungen von Direktinvestitionen auf die Nachhaltigkeit, Risikoaversion, Finanzwissen) sind ebenfalls wichtig, um die Entscheidung für nachhaltige Fonds zu erklären.

→ JEL classification: G53, G11, G41, C52, C91, A13
→ Keywords: portfolio choice, sustainable investments, Socially responsible investments, Ethical investing, Corporate social responsibility, equity funds, financial literacy

Introduction

Sustainable investment, which represents the financial investment processes additionally considering environmental, social, and corporate governance (ESG) issues, is fast-growing. The growth is driven by the desire of private investors assessing ESG aspects of firm conduct. The United Nations support sustainable investments and offer a guideline with six principles for responsible investments (UNPRI, 2021). The financial institutions face the pressure by their customers, investors and regulators to offer sustainable financial products. But then, there is widespread uncertainty about how private investors understand and evaluate sustainable investments. Many private and institutional investors who like the idea of financing sustainable investments, have only a vague idea about the concept of sustainability and how it relates to investment performance. In a survey among German adults, respondents indicated that they do not understand ESG financial products (64 %), do not understand the implementation of sustainability in the investment process and its relation to return and risk (50 %), and have not been referred to ESG financial investments by financial advisors (47 %) (Röstel, 2019). According to a survey of the DIA, only 14 % of respondents among institutional and private investors correctly understand the meaning of the term "sustainable financial investments", for about 19 % ESG criteria played a role in a past investment decision, 32 % are planning to consider ESG in future investment decisions and 77 % do not know any advisor for sustainable investments (Morgenstern, 2020). To the best of our knowledge, there is no validated scale for the measurement of the sustainable financial literacy and its relation to the actual investment process

The paper aims to measure and analyze sustainable financial preferences among young adults. In particular, we analyze whether the selection of ESG funds by young adults is driven by the fund attributes (e. g., expected return, risk, geographic focus), the socio-economic characteristics and/or behavioral latent characteristics. We focus on young adults, who are in the phase of forming their lives, because it offers a good opportunity to analyze the sustainable investment preferences of future generation. From a portfolio management perspective, the crucial step for the inclusion of sustainability into portfolio formation is investors' preferences for return, risk and sustainability (Gasser et al., 2017; Varmaz et al., 2021). We empirically analyze a concept how to measure the preferences for financial sustainability for the purpose of the portfolio management. We conduct a choice-based approach as an indirect preference elicitation approach which is shown to be more externally valid compared to direct methods (Louviere & Islam, 2008). In the choice-based experiment, the young adults can choose between conventional investment funds and sustainable investment funds (ESG funds). We examine how young adults prioritize investments between the elements of ESG funds when evaluating the investment performance with conventional funds to discern differences in preference heterogeneity. The heterogeneity of young adults may be relevant for the characterization of preferences for attributes of ESG funds. Lagerkvist et al. (2020a) point out that systematic preference heterogeneity can refer to observable variation in the characteristics of individuals (such as socio-economic, demographic or personal characteristics). Additionally, we model potentially unobserved characteristics of individuals by latent class choice models.

The analysis of sustainable preferences is important because they can lead to current or future real investments that contribute to the achievement of a sustainability goal, for example, reducing CO_2 emissions (Folqué et al., 2021; Wilkens & Klein, 2021). The global sustainability agenda, including the transition toward a low-carbon economy, has become an important factor for investors who demand comprehensive measurement of both, financial and ESG risks and opportunities in investment portfolios (Hübel & Scholz, 2020; Kumar et al., 2016). Consequently, the ESG investments are part of a transformation towards a sustainable economy. The financial investments will have a transformative effect if they lead to (current or future) realization of sustainable real investments. In theory, the effects of sustainable financial investments may be direct, e.g., by the means of green bonds, or indirect, e.g., by buying shares of sustainable firms or sustainable investment funds. This paper deals with indirect effects. The indirect effects are related either to the decrease in the cost of capital of refinancing for firms that actually conduct the sustainable real investments without green washing or to the increase of the cash flows generated by companys' sustainable products and services (Louche et al., 2019). According to the financial economics literature, the decrease in expected return is accompanied by an increase of the price for the sustainable investment.

The sustainable finance literature shows that the sustainable financial investors have more obstacles to overcome relative to conventional investors because the ESG funds differ across key dimensions as investment objective and investment style (Joliet & Titova, 2018). These differences make comparability among ESG funds as well as between ESG funds and conventional funds difficult. Benabou and Tirole (2010) argue that the ESG activity of a firm can have three objectives: 1. firms can "do well by doing good" (e.g., reducing workplace injury); 2. firms can maximize shareholder value when they exercise ESG behavior on behalf of stakeholders (e.g., customers paying more for high-priced fair trade products); 3. firms can destroy value when they engage in projects for the benefit of the managers. For example, Edmans (2011) shows that sustainable firms enjoy satisfied employees, good governance and loyal customers (Edmans, 2011). These firms generate higher than expected cash flows due to their greater efficiency. Hoepner et al. (2020) argue that companies with a high value of ESG characteristics relative to companies with low ESG values may attract investors seeking protection from legal, reputational, or operational challenges. These challenges may decrease the future cash flows for low ESG firms. Friede et al. (2015) conduct a meta-analysis of 60 meta studies including over 2000 single studies. They document that a small fraction of the studies finds a significantly negative relation between sustainability of a firm and its financial performance. However, as the sustainability includes a wide range of aspects it is difficult to conclude for investors how the sustainability of a firm will affect its expected return and risk. While the majority of theoretical literature suggests that the sustainability lowers expected returns, the empirical results are inconclusive. It follows that the evaluation process of ESG funds is more challenging for investors.

The results of our choice-based experiments suggest that consistent with the traditional financial economics literature, the trade-off between return and risk is also important in the selection of ESG funds for sustainable investors. Specifically, the likelihood of choosing an ESG fund increases with higher return and lower risk. Additionally, the ESG fund with a global geographic focus are likelier to be selected by the participants. Somewhat surprisingly, the financial literacy is not significantly related to the selection of an ESG fund. As the ESG funds available in our choice experiment have lower return relative to the conventional funds, we initially expected to see a decrease of likelihood to select an ESG fund for higher levels of the financial literacy. An explanation might be that even if participants have high financial literacy, they are willing to sacrifice return on investment for sustainability. Among the observable individual characteristics that might explain preference heterogeneity, the individual's concerns on sustainability and the individual's importance of direct impact of investments on ESG increase the likelihood of ESG fund selection. Additionally, participants preferring investments with low risk and environmental impact also prefer ESG funds.

The paper contributes to the literature by providing evidence from choice-based experiments how young adults choose among conventional and ESG funds. Specifically, we show the fund attributes that are important for the choice of young adults and the personal characteristics that increase the likelihood of selecting an ESG fund. The paper also relates to the measurement of sustainable financial literacy as we show that the participants are willing to forego returns in exchange for sustainability. The closest studies to ours is conducted by Apostolakis et al. (2016) and Lagerkvist et al. (2020). They study the preferences for sustainability of private investors and model the probability of the choice for ESG investments and funds characteristics, e. g., expected return, risk, sustainability focus. We complement their studies in regard to several dimensions. First, we include the financial literacy of participants in the choice model for ESG investments. Individuals cannot make informed choices when they do not understand the basics of financial investments and the relation between return and risk. Second, we include items about the awareness about sustainability and sustainable finance of participants because the literature proposes that this knowledge may affect the choice between conventional and sustainable products. Third, we include the beliefs of the participants about the return on ESG funds. While a wide range of theory papers in financial economics propose that the equilibrium relation between return and ESG needs to become negative, the empirical results suggest that the relation may be positive or at least non-negative (Friede et al., 2015). The control of beliefs of the participants is important because the ESG funds presented to the participants have lower expected return. Otherwise, we cannot discriminate in the choice experiment whether the ESG fund is selected due to the higher return or due to the ESG focus. Fourth, we also control for personal characteristics of the participants, e. g., logical thinking and personal traits.

The paper is organized as follows: in section 2, we give an overview of the relevant literature. Section 3 describes the data and the estimation method. We present the results and discussion in section 4, section 5 summarizes.

Literature Review

In this section, we present the variables that are perceived as important for sustainable investment decisions in the literature and discuss how the investment decision strategy of a person can be measured. Specifically, the concepts of sustainable financial literacy and sustainable investment strategies are discussed and an overview of various strands of literature is provided. Additionally, attitude and ESG beliefs as well as personal traits that have been proven to influence investment choice, namely conscientiousness, impulsivity, faith in intuition, and need for cognition are discussed. To empirically test the validity of theoretical concepts, it is important to quantify the variables under study in a way that is consistent with and appropriate for the theory.

The Concept of Sustainable Financial Literacy

The concept of sustainable financial literacy (SFL) is build up on the concept of financial literacy (FL). As in many areas of the social sciences, there is not yet a comprehensive, uniform, and universally accepted definition of financial literacy and sustainable financial literacy (Hung et al., 2009). Research agrees that it is a multidimensional concept, that is part of basic education and can be subject to factors as socio-demographic factors, individual behavior, education and training. PISA, an OECD program to measure and evaluate global education systems using the skills and competences of 15-year-olds, uses a two-part definition of financial literacy. The first part defines financial literacy as the knowledge and understanding of financial concepts and their risks and the ability (as well as motivation and confidence) to apply this knowledge to make effective financial decisions. The second part relates to the purpose of the skills and competencies, which is to increase prosperity for oneself and society and to participate in economic life (OECD, 2017a, 2017b). Previous literature (e.g., Chen & Volpe, 1998; Lusardi & Mitchell, 2007, 2008, 2014) uses financial literacy and financial knowledge as interchangeable concepts and build their concept on the definition of OECD.

Expanding the definition of financial literacy to incorporate the sustainability we use sustainable investment strategies, which describe financial investment processes additionally considering ESG issues. In particular, sustainable investments increase in the last years. According to the GSI-Alliance there is a 15 % increase from 2018 to the beginning of 2020. They identify that the most common ESG investment strategy applies negative screening (Global Sustainable Investment Alliance (GSIA), 2021). Climate change and negative environmental effects are increasing and shifting the focus more towards sustainable investments. Investors start to focus their efforts on areas where they can achieve positive environmental and social outcomes. Investors are able to influence corporate behavior and redirect capital to sustainable companies and projects. Even the financial market is not protected from the negative effects of climate change. By incorporating ESG considerations into their investment decisions, investors seek to both mitigate sustainability risks and enhance long-term returns (Bollen, 2007; Eurosif & Sakuma-Keck, 2021).

Sustainable Investment Strategies

The financial market is affected by climate change and sustainability transformation. The demand for investments with a social and/or environmental benefit increases (Eurosif & Sakuma-Keck, 2021; GIIN, 2019) and investment professionals are adopting sustainable investment practices (Busch et al., 2015; Friede et al., 2015). It is beyond dispute, that the benefit of a sustainable investment needs a quantification. But there is widespread uncertainty about how investors understand and evaluate sustainable investment portfolios. Previous literature often claims that the results of studies on the correlation between ESG and corporate financial performance are unclear or inconclusive and argue about the total effect (Borgers et al., 2013; Hoepner & McMillan, 2009; Orlitzky, 2011, 2013; Revelli & Viviani, 2015; van Beurden & Gössling, 2008; Wood, 2010). The study of Friede et al. (2015) provides an overview and the results of over 2000 empirical studies about the relation between ESG and corporate financial performance. Most studies focus on one aspect, either environmental, social or governance, a few on two parts, rarely all three (Friede et al., 2015). On average, Friede et al. (2015) report a non-negative correlation between ESG-criteria and the corporate financial performance in about 90 % of studies. On the other hand, Nilsson (2007) shows that there is no significant difference between the performance of a conventional investment and a sustainable investment. Auer and Schuhmacher (2016) report that, depending on framework of the analysis as ESG definition and sector, sustainable investments have not paid off for investors in Europe. Moreover, empirical research demonstrates that financial attributes are most often preferred over ESG attributes (Brimble et al., 2013). Regardless of the sustainable preferences, the financial performance criteria are most important for investors (Vyvyan et al., 2007). In addition, their results provide evidence of a behavior gap in environmental attitudes and investment choices.

The negative and positive screening is a common concept for sustainable investment strategies. Renneboog et al. (2008) describe that negative screening means removing specific funds or companies according to the ESG-criteria. The positive screening refers to a specific fund or company with superior ESG-criteria relative to industry peers. In line with Apostolakis et al. (2018), Matos (2020) and Lagerkvist et al. (2020b) our study integrates the following three different strategies: negative and positive screening as well as norm-based screening (Amel-Zadeh & Serafeim, 2017; CFA Institute, 2015). Besides the screening strategy, the engagement is also important: Investors can determine companies' direction towards or against ESG-criteria at general meetings (Lagerkvist et al., 2020b; Matos, 2020).

In line with Fishbein (2008), Gopinath (1995), and Lagerkvist et al. (2020b), we apply a reasoned action approach to describe the sustainable investment decisions of young adults. The preferences stated in the choice experiment along with the influence of skills, abilities and environmental constraints can explain sustainable financial decisions. Accordingly, the sustainable financial literacy and sustainable financial decisions are influenced by observable and latent variables. For example, past decision making and demographic aspects can describe future decisions. Latent variables refer to personal traits, attitudes, preferences, and risk aversion. The preference heterogeneity by observable and latent variables results in the choice behavior that is affected by knowledge of sustainable financial literacy and situational conditions (Fishbein, 2008; Gopinath, 1995; Lagerkvist et al., 2020b).

Personal Traits

The traditional economics theory is based on the rational decision making. However, personal traits can influence an investment choice as well. We consider conscientiousness, impulsivity, faith in intuition, and need for cognition in our study.

Conscientiousness

Conscientiousness refers to individual differences in the tendency to be hardworking, orderly, responsible to others, self-controlled, and rule abiding (Roberts et al., 2014). Research has shown that conscientiousness has an influence on pro-environmental behaviors like recycling (Simmons & Widmar, 2010) and energy saving (Milfont & Sibley, 2012). Yu and Yu (2017) demonstrate that conscientiousness is positively linked to pro-environmental attitude. Furthermore, research suggests that conscientiousness and investment behavior are related (Durand et al., 2013; Husnain et al., 2019; Letkiewicz & Fox, 2014; Tauni et al., 2017). Individuals high on conscientiousness have well-defined investment goals. Such individuals are structured, go for a systematic analysis, and also depict strong intentions to invest in long term investment portfolios (Mayfield et al., 2008).

Impulsivity: Urgency & Intention

The psychological construct impulsivity is one of the basic variables of research and diagnostics of behavioral control. Behavioral control, in turn, is very closely linked to the regulation of the individual's physical reality (Eysenck, n.d.). This includes the interaction of the individual with his environment; e.g., Zafar et al. (2021) show the link between impulsivity and sustainable purchase decisions. Further research demonstrates a link between risk preferences in the investment domain and impulsivity (Zaleskiewicz, 2001). Despite the diverse findings in the field, there is still no clear and unified definition of the construct (Kovaleva et al., 2012). It is assumed that the construct impulsivity is multidimensional to encompass various aspects of impulsive behavior. In this context, the *urgency* dimension captures impulsive behavior per se. The *intention* dimension captures the construct impulsivity in the opposite direction.

Faith in Intuition & Need for Cognition

In psychology, two modes of thinking and information processing are distinguished. The first mode has been called intuitive, emotional, heuristic, or experiential, and the second mode rational, analytical, objective, or logical. The Rational-Experiential Inventory (Epstein, 1996) was designed to measure individual differences in intuitive-experiential and analytical-rational thinking. The first subscale, *faith in intuition*, is a measure of confidence in one's intuitive abilities. The second subscale, *need for cognition*, reflects the engagement in intellectual activities. Research by Zaleskiewicz (2001) shows significant correlations between the dimensions and financial risk-taking behaviors. Especially, need for cognition has been associated with a tendency to assess the quality of information and to attend different viewpoints which may reduce cognitive biases, and increase an interest in scientific research (Feist, 2012; Petty et al., 2005; Tsfati & Cappella, 2010; Winter & Krämer, 2012). Vainio (2019) demonstrates that need for cognition is positively associated with pro-environmental behavior like eating less meat.

Attitude and ESG Beliefs

Ajzen (1991, 2011) demonstrates in his theory of planned behavior that behavior is a manifestation of values and attitudes of an individual. Individuals that express concern both for the welfare of others and for the environment show a more positive attitude towards social and environmental means (Hurst et al., 2013; Liobikiene & Juknys, 2016; Steg et al., 2014). Wachholz et al. (2014) report that most college students express environmental concerns. Drawing from the theory of planned behavior, studies support the precedence of a positive attitude towards environmental and social concerns and on sustainable behavioral intentions (Budovska et al., 2019; Chao, 2012; Greaves et al., 2013; Mancha & Yoder, 2015; Nigbur et al., 2010; Yu & Yu, 2017).

Data and Estimation Method

Data and Descriptive Statistics

Our data is collected from an anonymous online survey in October 2021 based on a sample of 104 students from the University of Applied Sciences Bremen. The survey includes 40 items in the experiment on investment decision, financial literacy, personal traits, risk aversion, demographics, attitudes to sustainability and mindset towards personal finances. The translated survey is in the online appendix. We approached the students via the mailing lists from the university and invited them to participate in the online survey. The students came from different study programs and are our proxy for the young adults. Out of about 6000 invited students, 198 accessed the survey (respond rate 3.3 %) and 104 completed the online survey in full. The descriptive statistics of our data sample are in Table 1.

Our sample include 49.05 % of female, 49.05 % male and 1.9 % students without gender orientation ('diverse'). The average age of student is 22.71, with female students being slightly younger. On average, the students are in their 3-rd term. We ask the students to self-assess their knowledge level about sustainable investment (variable Knowledge ESG) on a scale between 1 (never heard of) and 6 (very good). The average level is about 3.57. Female students self-report significantly higher levels of ESG knowledge relative to male students. We have two variables measuring the risk aversion in Table 1. The first variable (risk aversion 1) is the answer from a

Table 1

Descriptive statistics

	All	Female	Male	Diverse	t-Stat
Gender	100%	49.05%	49.05%	1.90%	-
Age	22.71	21.88	23.49	24.00	-
Term	3.19	3.00	3.22	7.00	-
Knowledge ESG (1 = never heard of, ..., 4 = average, ... 6= very good)	3.57	4.12	3.06	2.50	10.73
Risk aversion 1 (1 = prefers risk-free, 2 = prefers risky investments)	1.26	1.21	1.32	1.00	-1.99
Risk aversion 2 (1 = invest into high-risk projects, ..., 4 = take no risky projects)	2.72	3.06	2.38	3.50	10.00
Financial literacy	2.01	1.90	2.33	1.00	6.24
Important characteristics of investments (1= not important, 2 = somewhat important, 3 = very important)					
Return	2.34	2.23	2.49	1.00	-4.48
Risk	2.43	2.55	2.32	2.00	4.08
Environmental impact	2.05	2.04	2.02	3.00	0.30
Social impact	1.94	2.00	1.84	3.00	2.45

Note: The table gives an overview of self-reported characteristics of the participants in the online survey. The column All (Female, Male, Diverse) shows the values for all (female, male, diverse) students. The column t-Stat reports the t-statistics from the t-test of equal averages for the groups of female and male students. The variable **gender** shows the proportion of female, male and diverse students, respectively, in %. Age is the average age of the students. **Term** is the current study term of the students. In Germany, the academic year is divided into two terms and the regular study programs last 6 – 7 terms (equivalent to 3 – 3.5 study years). **Knowledge ESG** indicates how the students assess the individual level of knowledge about sustainable investments. The students are asked this question: "Equity funds focused on sustainability invest money in companies based on environmental, social and governance factors. Environmental factors include renewable energy, carbon dioxide emissions, natural resources, pollution and waste. Social factors include human rights, fair working conditions, health and safety, and the right to privacy. Governance factors include corporate governance, diversity, wage payment, business ethics, tax transparency, corruption, and instability. How would you rate your knowledge of sustainable investing?" **Risk aversion 1** and **risk aversion 2** are related to the willingness of the students to bear risk in exchange for higher return. For the variable risk aversion 1, the students are offered the choice between: 1. A sure win of 750 euros and 2. 40% chance to win 2000 euros and a 60% chance to win nothing. We assign the value 1 to the first option and value 2 to the second option. For the variable risk aversion, the students took position to "[w]hich of the statements comes closest to the financial risk you are willing to take when saving or investing? 1. I take a high financial risk and expect a high return, 2. I take above average financial risks and expect above average returns, 3. I take average financial risks and expect an average return, 4. I am not willing to take financial risk." **Financial literacy** is the average number of correctly answered 'Big Three' questions on financial literacy. Financial literacy includes questions on rate of return, inflation and diversification. **Important characteristics of investments** asks the students: "Imagine that you save a fixed amount every month, e.g., 50 euros. With this in mind, answer the following question. Which of the following characteristics of a project are important to you when you think about your monthly savings, i.e., which characteristics make an investment more attractive for you?" The students can state for each characteristic (return, risk, environmental impact, social impact) how important these are.

question with two options. The students are asked to decide whether they prefer a risk-free profit of 750 Euro (option 1) or a lottery with a probability of 40% to earn 2000 Euro, otherwise nothing (option 2). The second variable (risk aversion 2) indicates students' answer how much risk they accept when they invest. The options vary from high risk/high return to no risk at all, where higher values indicate higher risk aversion. For both variables, the female students in our sample are significantly more risk averse.

We measure the level of financial literacy by the 'Big Three' questions (Lusardi & Mitchell, 2014). These questions are widely and globally used to enhance the comparison across the studies on financial literacy (Arnold et al., 2018; Lusardi & Mitchell, 2014). The Big-Three are often considered as a standardized measure of financial literacy (Knoll & Houts, 2012). They include the questions of interest rates, inflation and risk diversification. The variable FL in Table 1 indicates the average number of correct answers to the 'Big Three' questions. On average, the students correctly solve two questions. The average number of correct answers is significantly lower for female students. The lower score on financial literacy for female students is in line with previous literature (Bucher-Koenen et al., 2017; Riebe, 2021).

The last part of Table 1 relates to the importance of selected investment characteristics for the students. The importance scale range is from 1 for not important to 3 for very important. Both, the return and risk are important and more important relative to environmental or social impact of the investments. For return and risk, we observe a gender difference. For female students, risk is more important and for male students, the return on investment is more important. The investment impact (environmental or social) is somewhat important for students. The social impact is significantly more important for female students.

Choice Experiment

For the experiment of the stated preference choices for sustainable financial investments, we follow the guidelines provided by Apostolakis et al. (2016) and Lagerkvist et al. (2020). At the beginning of the stated preference experiment, we show students an information section, which describes the characteristics of equity funds. We translate and adapt the description of characteristics of equity funds of Lagerkvist et al. (2020) to the German market. In particular, we convert the currency to Euro and the market focus to Germany.

We adapt the choice tasks from Lagerkvist et al. (2020) and change the choice task descriptions to meet the requirement of the German market. The students decide in 5 choice tasks. Each task includes three equity funds. An illustration of a task is presented in Table 2. For each equity fund, we provide the description of its attributes. The fund attributes include risk classification, expected return, management style and costs, geographical focus, sustainability focus and sustainability selection strategies. The attributes of equity funds vary in each task. We also provide detailed description of each attribute by clicking on a link in the survey. However, only 19 % of the students acquire the additional information. Each task includes a conventional equity fund without a sustainability focus. The conventional equity fund is a choice alternative, which may be familiar to student. We include the conventional fund because previous literature suggests that private investors invest in both ethical and conventional funds (Jansson & Biel, 2011; Michelson et al., 2004). We apply the cheap-talk script at the begin of the choice task exercises to mitigate hypothetical bias (e.g., inflated "willingness to pay") in stated preference elicitation and in particular for choice experiment (Penn & Hu, 2019).

In our choice experiment, the ESG investment funds must not have higher expected returns relative to the conventional investment funds. The reason is that otherwise we could not discriminate whether the students chose the fund due to the higher expected return as proposed by the traditional financial economics theory or due to their sustainability focus. We allow equal or lower returns for ESG funds (relative to conventional funds). The other attributes of the funds vary randomly between the tasks. Additionally, we control for the beliefs of the students about the expected return on ESG funds. If students think that ESG funds offer higher expected return relative to the conventional equity funds, the presented ESG funds with lower expected return could partially explain, why these students would not choose ESG funds.

Table 2

Illustration of a choice set within the stated preference section

	Investment fund 1	Investment fund 2	Investment fund 3
Management style	Passive management	Passive management	Active management
Management fee p. a.	0.40%	0.40%	1.10%
Risk classification	Risk category 5 ±10–15% variation per year	Risk category 5 ±10–15% variation per year	Risk category 7 more than 25% variation per year
Geographic focus	German equities	German equities	Global equities
Sustainability selection strategy	-	Negative screening: The investment fund excludes countries, sectors or companies that are not considered sustainable.	Positive screening: The investment fund actively selects companies that proactively work with sustainability.
Sustainability focus	None	Environment, e.g., climate, air pollution, renewable energy	Social, e.g., human rights, working conditions, job security
Expected annual return	13%	7%	13%

Note: The table gives an example of one choice task presented to the participants of our online survey. Participants could have accessed a detailed description of equity fund attributes. In each task, the participants can select an investment fund to invest 100 euro monthly for the time period of the next 10 years. We use the cheap-talk script to mitigate the hypothetical bias when choosing the investment fund. Specifically, at the start of the choice task, we presented the following introduction to the students: "Equity funds account for about 40% of total German fund assets. By saving in equity funds, you can diversify your savings into German or foreign investments. Saving in funds inevitably involves risk and when choosing equity funds you should weigh up what risk you are prepared to accept. Higher risk means greater risk of losing money, but also greater opportunity for higher returns. A lower risk, on the other hand, means lower chances of higher returns, but also a lower risk of loss. In both cases, total loss is excluded. The investment strategy and the selection of stocks for the fund are managed by professional investors and may be more or less computerized.
You will now be introduced to various features of equity funds.
Imagine that you decide to invest in a stock fund in which you save 100 euros per month. You may already be saving monthly in certain equity funds, but we ask you to choose the fund you would like to save in based on the specified conditions. Saving 100 euros per month over a period of 10 years may be challenging! Therefore, do your best to ensure that your choice of equity fund truly reflects what is important to you in your fund savings."

Measures of Heterogeneity in Choice Tasks

As measures of heterogeneity, we include financial literacy, logical thinking, sustainability concerns, personal traits, risk aversion, importance of ESG, attitude to savings, attitude to ESG investments and individual beliefs about return and risk of ESG funds.

Financial literacy is measured by the 'Big Three' questions that are also used in Table 1 (Riebe, 2021). The financial literacy refers to the understanding of financial investment and savings. The inclusion of the financial literacy aims to analyze whether the students understand the financial consequences of their choices. The traditional financial economics theory suggests a negative relation between financial literacy and selection of ESG funds. We include an auxiliary question on population exponential growth because the interest rate question from Big-Three has recently received broad media attention. Students may know the answer to the question from the media but not understand the reason. The population growth question is a multiple-choice question, where the students are asked: "The population of the colorful giant parrot grows by 10% every year. Starting from the population 100, the population of colorful giant parrot after 3 years will be closest to the following number".

Logical thinking describes the ability of students to analyze a problem and come up with a sensible solution. We extracted four questions from the German translation of the IQ test by Wechsler (1958). Since financial investment is associated with financial mathematics, the ability of logical thinking is potentially related to understanding of the mechanism of financial investments and long-term consequences of lower returns. As the expected return on ESG is lower in our experiment, according to the traditional financial economics theory we expect that logical thinking is negatively associated with the decision to select ESG funds.

Sustainability concerns addresses the individual relevance for sustainability problems (Apostolakis et al., 2016). These concerns may influence the willingness to forego return in exchange for sustainability. The literature argues that social concerns increase the probability of conscientious behavior for private investors (Jansson & Biel, 2011). We have included two questions measuring individuals' environmental and social concerns. We expect increased concerns about environmental and social issues to positively influence the choice of an ESG fund.

We follow the literature and include the psychological constructs conscientiousness (Körner et al., 2008), impulsivity (Kovaleva et al., 2012; Zaleskiewicz, 2001), faith in intuition and need for cognition (Keller et al., 2000) as personal traits. Each construct is measured with several items on a 5-point scale (1 = strongly disagree, 5 = strongly agree).

In financial economics literature, risk aversion indicates the trade-off between return and risk, i. e., how much risk is an investor willing to accept to gain an expected return. According to the financial theory, the higher the risk aversion is the lower is the accepted risk for a given level of expected return. Kapteyn and Teppa (2011) show that the ad-hoc measures about risk tolerance seem to explain very well the actual investment behavior of investors, i. e., the risk of the actual portfolios of the participants. In line with Apostolakis et al. (2016) and Kapteyn and Teppa (2011), our measure for risk aversion uses three items with a 5-point scale (1 = strongly disagree, 5 = strongly agree) reflecting the extent to which the individual is willing to be exposed to larger risks for larger financial gains. The financial economics literature proposes that the higher the risk aversion is the higher the expected return needs to be to motivate investors to invest into risky assets.

For the attitude to savings, the characteristic of investments and the importance of ESG, we follow Apostolakis et al. (2016). We measure attitude to saving in regard to private savings and the return on private savings. Characteristic of investments is measured by four general statements about the important aspects of personal investment in terms of return, risk, environmental and social impact. Importance of ESG (translated based on Apostolakis et al., 2016) is measured using 14 statements (1 = very unimportant; 7 = very important) related to the ESG criteria when choosing direct investment opportunities.

For individual beliefs about return of ESG funds, we ask the students to set the return on ESG investments in relation to conventional investment (1 = much less, 5 = much more). We expect that students, who estimate that ESG funds offer higher expected returns, chose less often ESG funds.

Estimation Method

Our estimation strategy to identify and quantify the effects of different dimensions of choice set complexity on choices follows DeShazo and Fermo (2002), Lagerkvist et al. (2020), and McFadden (1974). Accordingly, the utility function of student *i* from choosing equity fund *j* in the choice task *k* is

$$U_{ijk} = \beta^T \boldsymbol{x}_{ijk} + \varepsilon_{ijk}$$

where β is the parameter vector to be estimated, $\boldsymbol{x}$ is the vector of equity fund characteristics and ε is the *iid* extreme value type 1 distributed residuals with variance $\pi^2/6\lambda^2$, where the scale parameter λ equals $\lambda_i = \exp(\gamma' \boldsymbol{w}_i)$. $\boldsymbol{w}$ is a vector of descriptors of the student *i* and λ is the parameter vector to be estimated.

Assuming a linear utility model, the choice probabilities can be expressed as

$$P_{ijk} = \frac{\exp(\lambda(\beta^T \boldsymbol{x}_{ijk}))}{\sum_j^J \exp(\lambda(\beta^T \boldsymbol{x}_{ijk}))}$$

We estimate the parameters β and γ in a heteroscedastic conditional logit model (HCLM) via maximum likelihood estimator (McFadden, 1974). For the implementation, we follow the descriptions in Hill et al. (2018).

Results and Discussion

Table 3 presents our HCLM estimates for five specifications. The dependent variable is the choice of an investment fund. The fund characteristics return (net of management fee), risk and geographic investment focus are included in all specifications. The specifications vary in regard to the inclusion of students' characteristics (e.g., traits, attitudes, beliefs). The specification 5 includes all variables. The last three rows of Table 3 provide some information about model goodness of the fit. Adj. R2 is the adjusted R^2. The Log-Likelihood and the LR test statistics allow a comparison across the specifications. The addition of variance heterogeneity by personal characteristics in specifications 2–5 to the fund characteristics in specification 1 increases significantly the log-likelihood. We apply the LR test to compare the specifications 2–5 to the base specification 1. The LR test statistic is $LR = -2\ln\left(\frac{L(m_1)}{L(m_+)}\right)$, where L is the likelihood, m_1 refers to base specification and m_+ to the alternative. The test statistic LR is χ^2-distributed with the number of degrees of freedom equaling the number of additional variables in the alternative specification. Table 3 reports the LR test statistic (and not the p-value).

The results in Table 3 suggests that funds with lower risk and higher returns (net of management fees) are preferred by students. We find support that global investment focus is more preferred among the students suggesting that a home bias does not explain our results (Coval & Moskowitz, 1999; Lewis, 1999; Tesar & Werner, 1995). Moreover, the results suggest that funds with an environmental focus are likelier to be selected.

Table 3

Regression results

	1		2		3		4		5	
	coef	z	coef	z	coef	z	coef	z	coef	z
Fund characteristics										
Return	**0.51**	15.37	**0.56**	8.17	**0.51**	8.51	**0.50**	8.33	**0.54**	6.49
Risk	**-0.19**	9.90	**-0.22**	-4.59	**-0.20**	-4.42	**-0.19**	-4.08	**-0.24**	-4.21
Geog. focus global	**3.38**	-4.49	**3.46**	5.70	**3.36**	5.83	**3.68**	5.20	**3.89**	5.39
Financial literacy and Logical thinking										
Logical thinking			0.18	0.73					0.43	1.27
FL			-0.25	-0.91					-0.26	-0.74
Parrot growth			**-0.70**	-1.83					-0.43	-0.89
Important characteristics for investments										
High interest rate					0.06	0.14			0.51	0.90
Low risk					**1.33**	3.29			**1.57**	2.94
Environmental impact					**2.22**	3.51			**2.18**	2.97
Belief about ESG return										
Returns on ESG investment			-0.59	-1.41					-0.26	-0.47
Investment and ESG concerns										
Concerns banks			-0.35	-0.81					-0.68	-1.26
Concerns ESG			**1.59**	3.95					**0.94**	1.66
Importance of return on savings			0.11	0.27					0.83	1.41
Importance of savings			-0.26	-0.55					-0.69	-1.10
Attitude										
Attitude to ESG							0.40	1.01	-0.06	-0.13
Importance of ESG and impact of direct investments										
Important aspects of ESG							**0.88**	2.89	**0.48**	1.68
Risk aversion										
RA							**-1.19**	-2.28	-1.26	-1.51
Personal traits										
Conscientiousness							**-0.69**	-1.75	**-1.14**	-2.30
Urgency							0.33	1.17	-0.05	-0.15
Intent							0.05	0.22	-0.03	-0.11
Intuition							-0.43	-1.28	-0.41	-1.13
Need f. Cognition							-0.19	-0.59	0.26	0.56
Gender										
Female									0.14	0.35
Adj.R^2	0.31		0.34		0.38		0.33		0.34	
Log-Likelihood	-119		-106		-104		-93		-80	
LR test statistic			26.77		29.86		52.86		78.65	

Note: The table presents the estimated coefficients from the heteroscedastic conditional logit model for five specifications and their z-values as well as the measures of goodness of the fit (Adjusted R2, Log-Likelihood, LR test statistic from LR test comparing specifications 2–5 to basis specification 1). Bold values are significant at least at the 5% level. The variables are grouped in categories: Fund characteristics, financial literacy and logical thinking, important characteristics for investments, belief about ESG return, Investment and ESG concerns, attitude, importance of ESG and impact of direct investments, risk aversion, personal traits, gender. The corresponding questions and variables can be taken from the questionnaire in the appendix.

The financial literacy (FL) and the understanding of exponential growth (parrot population growth) are negatively associated with students' choice of ESG funds but FL is not significant. Moreover, the likelihood increases that students with higher values on the logical thinking test select an ESG fund. The students for whom low risk and environmental impact are important characteristics of an investment are significantly more likely to choose ESG funds. The risk aversion of students is negative but it is not a significant explanation of ESG fund selection.

There is some concern that the prior beliefs of some students about the return on ESG funds can drive the results. In the experiment, we only present ESG funds with lower or equal return relative to conventional funds. These students could be in favor for ESG funds but select the conventional funds because the return is higher. Our results suggest that the students believing that ESG funds offer higher return, were less likely to select ESG funds, however the coefficient is not significant.

Regarding investment and ESG concerns, only concerns on ESG dimensions (Concerns ESG) contribute positively and significantly to the selection of ESG funds. Positive attitude to ESG is insignificantly associated with ESG fund selection. Students who care about ESG and the impact of their direct investments clearly prefer ESG funds. Among personal traits, only conscientiousness seems to be significantly associated with choice of ESG funds. Need for cognition is reversely coded, i.e., higher values indicate lower need for cognition.

Our results suggest that ESG fund offerings can be created to fit personal characteristics of potential investors. First, individuals in our sample are valuing the trade-off between return and risk as proposed by the financial economics literature. The selection of an ESG fund increases with expected return and decreases with risk. Second, individuals are more likely to select an ESG fund when low risk and environmental orientation of the investments are important for them. Third, the direct impacts of the individual investment on sustainability are positively associated with the selection of an ESG fund.

The interpretation of our results is subject to several limitations. First, we do not observe the actual orders of private investors but the stated preferences of students as our proxy for young adults. For example, the risk as an inherent feature of financial investments is a limitation in our hypothetical setting. Our experimental design allows the inclusion of a wider and deeper set of attributes and levels of potential relevance to private ESG fund investors. Still, how the hypothetical choices influence the potentially inflated estimators of marginal utilities in Table 3 remains controversial in the literature. Previous literature on hypothetical biases suggests several approaches (e.g., cheap-talk script conducted in our study) to reduce the bias (e.g., Fifer et al., 2014). Second, in the implementation of the cheap-talk script we ask the students to choose ESG funds for a given amount of money (50 Euro) that is invested monthly. Clearly, the pre-set savings amount must not correspond to the preferences of the students.

Summary

We analyze stated preferences among students for sustainable fund investments. We have two observations to report. First, the trade-off between return and risk as postulated by the financial economics literature remains important. Global ESG funds with higher return and lower risk are preferred by students. Second, our results suggest that there are some latent factors (e.g., attitude, concerns, personal traits, financial literacy, risk aversion) that explain the stated preferences. We examine how observable and context-relevant characteristics of individual investors explain variance heterogeneity in their choice behavior. For example, students for whom investments with low risk and ESG impact is important, are more likely to select ESG funds. Similarly, students for whom ESG aspects of their direct investments are important, preferer ESG funds. Among personal traits, conscientiousness contributes significantly to the explanation of ESG fund selection. Our results suggest that sociodemographic characteristics do not explain the stated preferences but that latent student's characteristics are predictors of ESG fund selection. Apparently, students' selections are more likely to be driven by behavioral rather than by demographic characteristics.

References

— Ajzen, I. (2011): The theory of planned behaviour: Reactions and reflections. *https://doi.org/10.1080/08870446.2011.613995, 26*(9), 1113–1127. https://doi.org/10.1080/08870446.2011.613995.
— Amel-Zadeh, A. and G. Serafeim (2017): Why and How Investors Use ESG Information: Evidence from a Global Survey. *SSRN Electronic Journal.* https://doi.org/10.2139/SSRN.2925310.
— Apostolakis, G., F. Kraanen, and G. van Dijk (2016): Examining pension beneficiaries' willingness to pay for a socially responsible and impact investment portfolio: A case study in the Dutch healthcare sector. *Journal of Behavioral and Experimental Finance, 11,* 27–43. https://doi.org/10.1016/J.JBEF.2016.06.001.
— Apostolakis, G., G. van Dijk, F. Kraanen, and R. J. Blomme (2018): Examining socially responsible investment preferences: A discrete choice conjoint experiment. *Journal of Behavioral and Experimental Finance, 17,* 83–96. https://doi.org/10.1016/J.JBEF.2018.01.001.
— Auer, B. R. and F. Schuhmacher (2016): Do socially (ir)responsible investments pay? New evidence from international ESG data. *The Quarterly Review of Economics and Finance, 59,* 51–62. https://doi.org/10.1016/J.QREF.2015.07.002.
— Benabou, R. and J. Tirole (2010): Individual and Corporate Social Responsibility. *Economica,* 77(305), 1–19. https://doi.org/10.1111/J.1468-0335.2009.00843.X.
— Bollen, N. P. B. (2007): Mutual Fund Attributes and Investor Behavior. *Journal of Financial and Quantitative Analysis, 42*(3), 683–708. https://doi.org/10.1017/S0022109000004142.
— Borgers, A., J. Derwall, K. Koedijk, and J. ter Horst (2013): Stakeholder relations and stock returns: On errors in investors' expectations and learning. *Journal of Empirical Finance, 22,* 159–175. https://doi.org/10.1016/J.JEMPFIN.2013.04.003.
— Brimble, M., V. Vyvyan, and C. Ng (2013): Belief and Investing: Preferences and Attitudes of the Faithful. *Australasian Accounting, Business and Finance Journal,* 7(1), 23–41. https://doi.org/10.14453/aabfj.v7i1.3.
— Bucher-Koenen, T., A. Lusardi, R. Alessie, and M. van Rooij (2017): How Financially Literate Are Women? An Overview and New Insights. *Journal of Consumer Affairs, 51*(2), 255–283. https://doi.org/10.1111/joca.12121.
— Budovska, V., A. Torres Delgado, and T. Øgaard (2019): Pro-environmental behaviour of hotel guests: Application of the Theory of Planned Behaviour and social norms to towel re-use. *https://doi.org/10.1177/1467358419831431, 20*(1), 105–116. https://doi.org/10.1177/1467358419831431.
— Busch, T., R. Bauer, and M. Orlitzky (2015): Sustainable Development and Financial Markets: Old Paths and New Avenues. *http://dx.doi.org/10.1177/0007650315570701, 55*(3), 303–329. https://doi.org/10.1177/0007650315570701.

— CFA Institute (2015): *Environmental, Social, and Governance Issues in Investing: A Guide for Investment Professionals.* https://www.cfainstitute.org/-/media/documents/article/position-paper/esg-issues-in-investing-a-guide-for-investment-professionals.ashx.

— Chao, Y. L. (2012): Predicting people's environmental behaviour: theory of planned behaviour and model of responsible environmental behaviour. *http://dx.doi.org/10.1080/13504622.2011.634970, 18*(4), 437–461. https://doi.org/10.1080/13504622.2011.634970.

— Chen, H. and R. P. Volpe (1998): An analysis of personal financial literacy among college students. *Financial Services Review,* 7(2), 107–128. https://doi.org/10.1016/S1057-0810(99)80006-7.

— Coval, J. D. and T. J. Moskowitz (1999): Home Bias at Home: Local Equity Preference in Domestic Portfolios. *The Journal of Finance,* 54(6), 2045–2073. https://doi.org/10.1111/0022-1082.00181.

— DeShazo, J. R. and G. Fermo (2002). Designing Choice Sets for Stated Preference Methods: The Effects of Complexity on Choice Consistency. *Journal of Environmental Economics and Management,* 44(1), 123–143. https://doi.org/10.1006/JEEM.2001.1199.

— Durand, R., R. Newby, K. Tant, and S. Trepongkaruna (2013): Overconfidence, overreaction and personality. *Review of Behavioral Finance,* 5(2), 104–133. https://doi.org/10.1108/RBF-07-2012-0011/FULL/PDF.

— Edmans, A. (2011): Does the stock market fully value intangibles? Employee satisfaction and equity prices. *Journal of Financial Economics, 101*(3), 621–640. https://doi.org/10.1016/j.jfineco.2011.03.021.

— Epstein, S. (1996): Individual Differences in Intuitive-Experiential and Analytical-Rational Thinking Styles. *Article in Journal of Personality and Social Psychology.* https://doi.org/10.1037/0022-3514.71.2.390.

— Eurosif and K. Sakuma-Keck (2021): *Fostering Investor Impact Placing it at the heart of sustainable finance.* https://www.eurosif.org/news/eurosif-report-2021/.

— Eysenck, H. J. (n.d.): *Crime and personality.* 225. https://books.google.com/books/about/Crime_and_Personality.html?id=dihzoAEACAAJ.

— Feist, G. J. (2012): Predicting interest in and attitudes toward science from personality and need for cognition. *Personality and Individual Differences,* 52(7), 771–775. https://doi.org/10.1016/J.PAID.2012.01.005.

— Fifer, S., J. Rose, and S. Greaves (2014): Hypothetical bias in Stated Choice Experiments: Is it a problem? And if so, how do we deal with it? *Transportation Research Part A: Policy and Practice, 61,* 164–177. https://doi.org/10.1016/J.TRA.2013.12.010.

— Fishbein, M. (2008): A reasoned action approach to health promotion. *Medical Decision Making, 28*(6), 834–844. https://doi.org/10.1177/0272989X08326092.

— Folqué, M., E. Escrig-Olmedo, and T. Corzo Santamaría (2021): Sustainable development and financial system: Integrating ESG risks through sustainable investment strategies in a climate change context. *Sustainable Development, 2021,* 1–15. https://doi.org/10.1002/sd.2181.

— Friede, G., T. Busch, and A. Bassen (2015): ESG and financial performance: aggregated evidence from more than 2000 empirical studies. *Journal of Sustainable Finance and Investment,* 5(4), 210–233. https://doi.org/10.1080/20430795.2015.1118917.

— Gasser, S. M., M. Rammerstorfer, and K. Weinmayer (2017): Markowitz revisited: Social portfolio engineering. *European Journal of Operational Research, 258*(3), 1181–1190. https://doi.org/10.1016/j.ejor.2016.10.043.

— GIIN (2019): *Core characteristics of impact investing. Global Impact Investing Network.* https://thegiin.org/assets/Core%20Characteristics_webfile.pdf.

- Global Sustainable Investment Alliance (GSIA) (2021): *Global Sustainable Investment Review 2020*. http://www.gsi-alliance.org/trends-report-2020/.
- Gopinath, D. A. (1995): *Modeling heterogeneity in discrete choice processes : application to travel demand*.
- Greaves, M., L. D. Zibarras, and C. Stride (2013): Using the theory of planned behavior to explore environmental behavioral intentions in the workplace. *Journal of Environmental Psychology, 34*, 109–120. https://doi.org/10.1016/J.JENVP.2013.02.003.
- Hill, R. C., W. E. Griffiths, and G. C. Lim (2018): *Principles of econometrics* (5th ed.). Wiley. https://www.wiley.com/en-us/Principles+of+Econometrics%2C+5th+Edition-p-9781119320944.
- Hoepner, A. G. F. and D. G. McMillan (2009): Research on "Responsible Investment": An Influential Literature Analysis Comprising a Rating, Characterisation, Categorisation and Investigation. *SSRN Electronic Journal*. https://doi.org/10.2139/SSRN.1454793.
- Hoepner, A. G. F., I. Oikonomou, Z. Sautner, L. T. Starks, and X. Zhou (2020): ESG Shareholder Engagement and Downside Risk. In *SSRN Electronic Journal*. European Corporate Governance Institute – Finance Working Paper No. 671/2020. https://doi.org/10.2139/ssrn.2874252.
- Hübel, B. and H. Scholz (2020): Integrating sustainability risks in asset management: the role of ESG exposures and ESG ratings. *Journal of Asset Management, 21*(1), 52–69. https://doi.org/10.1057/s41260-019-00139-z.
- Hung, A., A. M. Parker, and J. Yoong (2009): Defining and Measuring Financial Literacy. *SSRN Electronic Journal, 708*, 28 pp. https://doi.org/10.2139/ssrn.1498674.
- Hurst, M., H. Dittmar, R. Bond, and T. Kasser (2013): The relationship between materialistic values and environmental attitudes and behaviors: A meta-analysis. *Journal of Environmental Psychology, 36*, 257–269. https://doi.org/10.1016/J.JENVP.2013.09.003.
- Husnain, B., S. Zulfiqar, A. Shah, and T. Fatima (2019): Effect of Neuroticism, Conscientiousness on Investment Decisions. Mediation Analysis of Financial Self-Efficacy 1 2 3. *CURJ, 09*, 15–26.
- Jansson, M. and A. Biel (2011): Motives to engage in sustainable investment: a comparison between institutional and private investors. *Sustainable Development, 19*(2), 135–142. https://doi.org/10.1002/SD.512.
- Joliet, R. and Y. Titova (2018): Equity SRI funds vacillate between ethics and money: An analysis of the funds' stock holding decisions. *Journal of Banking & Finance, 97*, 70–86. https://doi.org/10.1016/J.JBANKFIN.2018.09.011.
- Kapteyn, A. and F. Teppa (2011): Subjective measures of risk aversion, fixed costs, and portfolio choice. *Journal of Economic Psychology, 32*(4), 564–580. https://doi.org/10.1016/J.JOEP.2011.04.002.
- Keller, J., G. Bohner, and H. P. Erb (2000): Intuitive and Heuristic Judgment – Different Processes? Presentation of a German Version of the Rational-Experiential Inventory and of New Self-Report Scales of Heuristic Use. *Zeitschrift Fur Sozialpsychologie, 31*(2), 87–101. https://doi.org/10.1024//0044-3514.31.2.87.
- Körner, A., M. Geyer, M. Roth, M. Drapeau, G. Schmutzer, C. Albani, S. Schumann, and E. Brähler (2008): Personality assessment with the NEO-Five-Factor Inventory: The 30-item-short-version (NEO-FFI-30). *PPmP Psychotherapie Psychosomatik Medizinische Psychologie, 58*(6), 238–245. https://doi.org/10.1055/S-2007-986199/ID/22.
- Kovaleva, A., C. Beierlein, C. J. Kemper, and B. Rammstedt (2012): *Eine Kurzskala zur Messung von Impulsivität nach dem UPPS-Ansatz : Die Skala Impulsives-Verhalten-8 (I-8)* (No. 20).

GESIS – Leibniz-Institut für Sozialwissenschaften. https://www.gesis.org/fileadmin/upload/forschung/publikationen/gesis_reihen/gesis_arbeitsberichte/WorkingPapers_2012-20.pdf.
— Kumar, A., C. Smith, L. Badis, N. Wang, P. Ambrosy, and R. Tavares (2016): ESG factors and risk-adjusted performance: a new quantitative model. *Journal of Sustainable Finance & Investment, 6*(4), 292–300. https://doi.org/10.1080/20430795.2016.1234909.
— Lagerkvist, C. J., A. K. Edenbrandt, I. Tibbelin, and Y. Wahlstedt (2020): Preferences for sustainable and responsible equity funds – A choice experiment with Swedish private investors. *Journal of Behavioral and Experimental Finance, 28*, 100406. https://doi.org/10.1016/J.JBEF.2020.100406.
— Letkiewicz, J. C. and J. J. Fox (2014): Conscientiousness, Financial Literacy, and Asset Accumulation of Young Adults. *Journal of Consumer Affairs, 48*(2), 274–300. https://doi.org/10.1111/JOCA.12040.
— Lewis, K. K. (1999): Trying to Explain Home Bias in Equities and Consumption. *Journal of Economic Literature, 37*(2), 571–608. https://doi.org/10.1257/JEL.37.2.571.
— Liobikiene, G. and R. Juknys (2016): The role of values, environmental risk perception, awareness of consequences, and willingness to assume responsibility for environmentally-friendly behaviour: the Lithuanian case. *Journal of Cleaner Production, 112*, 3413–3422. https://doi.org/10.1016/J.JCLEPRO.2015.10.049.
— Louche, C., T. Busch, P. Crifo, and A. Marcus (2019): Financial Markets and the Transition to a Low-Carbon Economy: Challenging the Dominant Logics. *Organization and Environment, 32*(1), 3–17. https://doi.org/10.1177/1086026619831516.
— Louviere, J. J. and T. Islam (2008): A comparison of importance weights and willingness-to-pay measures derived from choice-based conjoint, constant sum scales and best-worst scaling. *Journal of Business Research, 61*(9), 903–911. https://doi.org/10.1016/J.JBUSRES.2006.11.010.
— Lusardi, A. and O. S. Mitchell (2007): Financial Literacy and Retirement Planning: New Evidence from the Rand American Life Panel. *SSRN Electronic Journal, 23*(4), 234–262. https://doi.org/10.2139/ssrn.1095869.
— Lusardi, A. and O. S. Mitchell (2008): Planning and financial literacy: How do women fare? *American Economic Review*. https://doi.org/10.1257/aer.98.2.413.
— Lusardi, A. and O. S. Mitchell (2014): The Economic Importance of Financial Literacy: Theory and Evidence. *Journal of Economic Literature, 52*(1), 5–44. https://doi.org/10.1257/JEL.52.1.5.
— Mancha, R. M. and C. Y. Yoder (2015): Cultural antecedents of green behavioral intent: An environmental theory of planned behavior. *Journal of Environmental Psychology, 43*, 145–154. https://doi.org/10.1016/J.JENVP.2015.06.005.
— Matos, P. (2020): ESG and Responsible Institutional Investing Around the World: A Critical Review. *SSRN Electronic Journal*. https://doi.org/10.2139/SSRN.3668998.
— Mayfield, C., G. Perdue, and K. Wooten (2008): *Investment management and personality type*.
— McFadden, D. (1974): The measurement of urban travel demand. *Journal of Public Economics, 3*(4), 303–328. https://doi.org/10.1016/0047-2727(74)90003-6.
— Michelson, G., N. Wailes, S. van der Laan, and G. Frost (2004): Ethical Investment Processes and Outcomes. *Journal of Business Ethics 2004 52:1, 52*(1), 1–10. https://doi.org/10.1023/B:BUSI.0000033103.12560.BE.
— Milfont, T. L. and C. G. Sibley (2012): The big five personality traits and environmental engagement: Associations at the individual and societal level. *Journal of Environmental Psychology, 32*(2), 187–195. https://doi.org/10.1016/J.JENVP.2011.12.006.

— Morgenstern, K. (2020): Wie halten es die Anleger mit der Nachhaltigkeit? *Deutsches Institut Für Altersvorsorge, o. V.*, 1–72. https://www.dia-vorsorge.de/wp-content/uploads/2020/08/DIA-Studie_Wie_halten_es_die_Anleger_mit_der_Nachhaltigkeit.pdf.
— Nigbur, D., E. Lyons, and D. Uzzell (2010): Attitudes, norms, identity and environmental behaviour: Using an expanded theory of planned behaviour to predict participation in a kerbside recycling programme. *British Journal of Social Psychology*, *49*(2), 259–284. https://doi.org/10.1348/014466609X449395.
— Nilsson, J. (2007): Investment with a Conscience: Examining the Impact of Pro-Social Attitudes and Perceived Financial Performance on Socially Responsible Investment Behavior. *Journal of Business Ethics*, *83*(2), 307–325. https://doi.org/10.1007/S10551-007-9621-Z.
— OECD (2017a): PISA 2015 Assessment and Analytical Framework: Science, Reading, Mathematic, Financial Literacy and Collaborative Problem Solving. *Pisa 2015*. https://doi.org/10.1596/28293.
— OECD (2017b): *PISA 2015 Results (Volume IV)*. OECD. https://doi.org/10.1787/9789264270282-en.
— Orlitzky, M. (2011): Institutional Logics in the Study of Organizations: The Social Construction of the Relationship between Corporate Social and Financial Performance. *Business Ethics Quarterly*, *21*(3), 409–444. https://doi.org/10.5840/BEQ201121325.
— Orlitzky, M. (2013): Corporate Social Responsibility, Noise, and Stock Market Volatility. *https://doi.org/10.5465/Amp.2012.0097*, *27*(3), 238–254. https://doi.org/10.5465/AMP.2012.0097.
— Penn, J. and W. Hu (2019): Cheap talk efficacy under potential and actual Hypothetical Bias: A meta-analysis. *Journal of Environmental Economics and Management*, *96*, 22–35. https://doi.org/10.1016/J.JEEM.2019.02.005.
— Petty, R. E., J. T. Cacioppo, A. J. Strathman, and J. R. Priester (2005): To Think or Not to Think: Exploring Two Routes to Persuasion. In *Persuasion: Psychological insights and perspectives*, 2nd ed. (pp. 81–116). Sage Publications, Inc.
— Renneboog, L., J. ter Horst, and C. Zhang (2008): The price of ethics and stakeholder governance: The performance of socially responsible mutual funds. *Journal of Corporate Finance*, *14*(3), 302–322. https://doi.org/10.1016/J.JCORPFIN.2008.03.009.
— Revelli, C. and J. L. Viviani (2015): Financial performance of socially responsible investing (SRI): what have we learned? A meta-analysis. *Business Ethics: A European Review*, *24*(2), 158–185. https://doi.org/10.1111/BEER.12076.
— Riebe, K. (2021): Determinants of Financial Literacy Among German Students – An Empirical Analysis. *Vierteljahrshefte Zur Wirtschaftsforschung*, *89*(4), 39–54. https://doi.org/10.3790/VJH.89.4.39.
— Roberts, B. W., C. Lejuez, R. F. Krueger, J. M. Richards, and P. L. Hill (2014): What is conscientiousness and how can it be assessed? *Developmental Psychology*, *50*(5), 1315–1330. https://doi.org/10.1037/A0031109.
— Röstel, D. (2019): Wie sicher ist nachhaltig? *BaFin Journal, Juni*, 25–30. https://www.bafin.de/SharedDocs/Veroeffentlichungen/DE/Fachartikel/2019/fa_bj_1906_nachhaltige_Geldanlage.html.
— Simmons, D. and R. Widmar (2010): Motivations and Barriers to Recycling: Toward a Strategy for Public Education. http://dx.doi.org/10.1080/00958964.1990.9943041, *22*(1), 13–18. https://doi.org/10.1080/00958964.1990.9943041.
— Steg, L., J. W. Bolderdijk, K. Keizer, and G. Perlaviciute (2014): An Integrated Framework for Encouraging Pro-environmental Behaviour: The role of values, situational factors and goals.

Journal of Environmental Psychology, 38, 104–115. https://doi.org/10.1016/J.JENVP.2014.01.002.
— Tauni, M. Z., H. X. Fang, and A. Iqbal (2017): The role of financial advice and word-of-mouth communication on the association between investor personality and stock trading behavior: Evidence from Chinese stock market. *Personality and Individual Differences, 108*, 55–65. https://doi.org/10.1016/J.PAID.2016.11.048.
— Tesar, L. L. and I. M. Werner (1995): Home bias and high turnover. *Journal of International Money and Finance, 14*(4), 467–492. https://doi.org/10.1016/0261-5606(95)00023-8.
— Tsfati, Y. and J. N. Cappella (2010): Why Do People Watch News They Do Not Trust? The Need for Cognition as a Moderator in the Association Between News Media Skepticism and Exposure. *http://dx.doi.org/10.1207/S1532785XMEP0703_2*, 7(3), 251–271. https://doi.org/10.1207/S1532785XMEP0703_2.
— UNPRI (2021): *What are the Principles for Responsible Investment? | PRI Web Page | PRI.* https://www.unpri.org/pri/what-are-the-principles-for-responsible-investment.
— Vainio, A. (2019): How consumers of meat-based and plant-based diets attend to scientific and commercial information sources: Eating motives, the need for cognition and ability to evaluate information. *Appetite, 138*, 72–79. https://doi.org/10.1016/J.APPET.2019.03.017.
— van Beurden, P. and T. Gössling (2008): The Worth of Values – A Literature Review on the Relation Between Corporate Social and Financial Performance. *Journal of Business Ethics, 82*(2), 407–424. https://doi.org/10.1007/S10551-008-9894-X.
— Varmaz, A., C. Fieberg, and T. Poddig (2021): Portfolio optimization for sustainable investments. *SSRN Electronic Journal.* https://doi.org/10.2139/SSRN.3859616.
— Vyvyan, V., C. Ng, and M. Brimble (2007): Socially Responsible Investing: the green attitudes and grey choices of Australian investors. *Corporate Governance: An International Review, 15*(2), 370–381. https://doi.org/10.1111/J.1467-8683.2007.00567.X.
— Wachholz, S., N. Artz, and D. Chene (2014): Warming to the idea: University students' knowledge and attitudes about climate change. *International Journal of Sustainability in Higher Education, 15*(2), 128–141. https://doi.org/10.1108/IJSHE-03-2012-0025/FULL/PDF.
— Wechsler, D. (1958): The Measurement and Appraisal of Adult Intelligence. In *The Measurement and Appraisal of Adult Intelligence* (4th ed.). Williams & Wilkins Co. https://doi.org/10.1037/11167-000.
— Wilkens, M. and C. Klein (2021): *Welche transformativen Wirkungen können nachhaltige Geldanlagen durch Verbraucherinnen und Verbraucher haben?* (Gutachten für den Verbraucherzentralen und Verbraucherverbände).
— Winter, S. and N. C. Krämer (2012): Selecting Science Information in Web 2.0: How Source Cues, Message Sidedness, and Need for Cognition Influence Users' Exposure to Blog Posts. *Journal of Computer-Mediated Communication, 18*(1), 80–96. https://doi.org/10.1111/J.1083-6101.2012.01596.X.
— Wood, D. J. (2010): Measuring Corporate Social Performance: A Review. *International Journal of Management Reviews, 12*(1), 50–84. https://doi.org/10.1111/J.1468-2370.2009.00274.X.
— Yu, T. Y. and T. K. Yu, (2017): The Moderating Effects of Students' Personality Traits on Pro-Environmental Behavioral Intentions in Response to Climate Change. *International Journal of Environmental Research and Public Health, 14*(12), 1472. https://doi.org/10.3390/IJERPH14121472.
— Zafar, A. U., J. Shen, M. Shahzad, and T. Islam (2021): Relation of impulsive urges and sustainable purchase decisions in the personalized environment of social media. *Sustainable Production and Consumption, 25*, 591–603. https://doi.org/10.1016/J.SPC.2020.11.020.

— Zaleskiewicz, T. (2001): Beyond risk seeking and risk aversion: personality and the dual nature of economic risk taking. *European Journal of Personality*, 15(S1), S105–S122. https://doi.org/10.1002/PER.426.

Appendix

Translation of the German Questionnaire

Q1. Are you ...

☐ female ☐ male ☐ diverse

Q2. How old are you?

Answer: (17 to 99)

Q3. In which study program are you enrolled?

Sustainable Financial Literacy

Imagine that you save a fixed amount every month, e. g., in the amount of 50 euros. With this in mind, please answer the following question.

Q4. Which of the following characteristics of a project are important to you when you think about your monthly savings, i. e., which characteristics make an investment more attractive? (adapted from Siemroth & Hornuf, 2021)

Sufficiently high interest rate
Low risk
Positive environmental impact (e. g., company reduces "CO2"; recycles a lot)
Positive social impact (e. g., product helps students to find housing)

(1 = unimportant, 2 = rather important, 3 = very important)

Below we ask you some questions about sustainable investments. Equity funds that focus on sustainability invest in companies based on environmental, social and governance criteria.

Environmental factors include renewable energy, carbon dioxide emissions, natural resources, pollution, and waste. Social factors include human rights, fair working conditions, health and safety, and the right to privacy. Governance factors include corporate governance, diversity, wage payment, business ethics, tax transparency, corruption, and instability.

Q5. How would you rate your knowledge of sustainable investments? (Brunen & Laubach, 2021)

☐ I have never heard of it ☐ Very low ☐ Low ☐ Average ☐ Good ☐ Very good

Q6 – Q10. Select an equity fund for your monthly savings (Lagerkvist et al., 2020)

Please read the following text carefully:

Equity funds account for about 40 % of total German fund assets. By saving in equity funds, you can diversify your savings into German or foreign investments. Saving in funds inevitably involves risk and when choosing equity funds you should weigh up what risk you are prepared to accept. Higher risk means greater risk of losing money, but also greater opportunity for higher returns. A lower risk, on the other hand, means lower chances of higher returns, but also a lower risk of loss. In both cases, total loss is excluded. The investment strategy and the selection of stocks for the fund are managed by professional investors and may be more or less computerized.

You will now be introduced to various features of equity funds.

Imagine that you decide to invest in a stock fund in which you save 100 euros per month, with the money to be used only after 10 years. You may already be saving monthly in certain equity funds, but we ask you to choose the fund you would like to save in based on the specified conditions. Saving 100 euros per month over a 10-year period may, for a variety of reasons, be a challenge! So do your best to ensure that your choice of equity fund truly reflects what is important to you in your fund savings.

We now present you with three funds with different characteristics to choose from. Choose which of the three you prefer in each case, when only these three are available for selection.

[*in total 5 choice sets per respondent*]

Q11. How high do you estimate the return of sustainable investments in comparison to investments without sustainability reference? (modified from Brunen & Laubach, 2021)

☐ much lower ☐ a little less ☐ the same ☐ a little higher ☐ much higher ☐ I don't know.

Investment and Sustainability Concerns (Apostolakis et al., 2016)

Imagine that you save a fixed amount every month, e. g. in the amount of 50 euros. With this in mind, answer the following question.

Q12. Do you worry about what happens to your money when you "take it to the bank", i. e. save it?

☐ Yes, very often. ☐ Yes, on a regular basis. ☐ Yes, sometimes. ☐ No, almost never. ☐ No, never.
☐ I don't know.

Q13. Are you concerned about climate change, human rights or pollution?

☐ Yes, very often. ☐ Yes, on a regular basis. ☐ Yes, sometimes. ☐ No, almost never. ☐ No, never.
☐ I don't know.

Attitude to Savings *(Q14. and Q15 from Apostolakis et al., 2016; Lagerkvist et al., 2020)*

Q14. How important is the return on your personal savings to you?

☐ Not at all important ☐ Somewhat important ☐ Relatively important ☐ Very important ☐ Extremely important

Q15. How important are your personal savings for you?

☐ Not at all important ☐ Somewhat important ☐ Relatively important ☐ Very important ☐ Extremely important

Q16. How do you personally rate yourself: Are you someone who is basically willing to do without something today in order to benefit from it in the future, or are you not willing to do so?

Please answer using the following scale: 0 = I would definitely not do without something today – to – 10 = I am very willing to do without something today.

Importance of SRI and Impact of Direct Investments *(Apostolakis et al., 2016; Lagerkvist et al., 2020)*

Imagine that you save a fixed amount every month, e.g. in the amount of 50 euros. With this in mind, answer the following question.

Q17. How important do you consider investments in ...?

☐ Not at all important ☐ Somewhat important ☐ Relatively important ☐ Very important ☐ Extremely important

Companies that engage in the local community through donations to worthy causes and employee volunteerism.
Companies that promote good employee relations.
Technologies that aim to improve transportation and infrastructure.
Companies that are not involved in human rights violations.
Companies that promote human rights standards.
Companies that work to protect the environment and are committed to recycling and waste reduction.
Companies that are not involved in oil exploration or mining.
Companies that work with efficient water management.
Companies that do not violate international norms and standards.
Companies that do not deal with weapons, alcohol, tobacco and pornography.
Companies that have nothing to do with nuclear power.
Companies that are committed to sustainability.
Technical innovations that contribute to a reduction in CO_2 emissions in the form of alternative energy sources and efficient use of natural resources.
Medical innovations and research for new treatments and medicines.

Attitude Scale

Q18. What do you think about investing in equity funds with a focus on sustainability?

1 = bad 2 3 4 5 = good
1 = careless 2 3 4 5 = useful
1 = uncertain 2 3 4 5 = certain
1 = not preferred 2 3 4 5 = preferred
1 = negative 2 3 4 5 = beneficial

Risk Aversion (Apostolakis et al., 2016; Brunen & Laubach, 2021; Lagerkvist et al., 2020)

Q19. Please rate the following statements:
1 = strongly disagree 5 = strongly agree

I am increasingly convinced that I should take greater financial risks in order to improve my financial situation.
If I believe an investment will be profitable, I am willing to borrow money to make that investment.
I am willing to risk losing money if there is also a chance to make money.

Q20. Which of the statements comes closest to the financial risk you are willing to take when saving or investing?

I take a high financial risk and expect a high return.
I take above average financial risks and expect above average returns. I take average financial risks and expect an average return.
I am not willing to take financial risk.

Q21. You have the choice between the following two options. Please choose one!

A safe return of 750 euros.
A 40 % chance to win 2000 euros and a 60 % chance to win nothing.

Financial Literacy (Big Three) (Lusardi & Mitchell, 2014; Riebe, 2021)

Q22. Suppose you have 100 euros in a savings account and the interest rate is 2 % per year. How much do you think you would have in the account after 5 years if you left the money in the savings account?

More than 110 euros
Exactly 110 euros
Less than 110 euros
I don't know.

Q23. Imagine that the interest rate on your savings account was 1 % per year and inflation was 2 % per year. After 1 year, could you afford to live on the money in this account ...

... more than you can buy today.
... buy exactly the same as today.
... buy less than today.
I don't know.

Q24. Imagine the following situation. You have 1000 Euros that you want to save with a high return and as little price fluctuation as possible for at least 3 years. Is the following statement true or false? Please estimate.

"Buying stock in a single company usually provides a safer return than stock mutual funds."
True, False, I don't know.

Q25. Imagine that you save a fixed amount each month for long-term goals. Which of the following forms of savings would you use?

Please indicate below how your savings would be divided:
To do so, check the form of saving and indicate in the free text field below how it is divided in percentage points. E.G.: Savings account 50, capital security 30, direct share investment 20.

Savings account in %
Securities savings with investment funds (e.g. equity funds, ETFs) in %
Direct investment in investment funds in %
Private fund insurance in %
Endowment insurance in %
Direct investment in equities in %

Understanding of Exponential Growth

Q26. The population of the giant parrot grows by 10 % every year. Starting from the population 100, the population of giant parrot after 3 years will be the closest to the following number: 130, 131, 132, 133.

Personal Traits (Keller et al., 2000; Körner et al., 2008; Kovaleva et al., 2012)

Q27. On this page you will find a number of statements that people can use to describe themselves. Read each statement and decide whether it fits you or not.
1 = strongly disagree 5 = strongly agree

I keep my things neat and clean.
I can manage my time quite well so that I finish my affairs on time.
I try to do all the tasks assigned to me very diligently.
When I make a commitment, I can definitely be counted on.
Sometimes I do things spontaneously that I would have been better off not doing.
To feel better, sometimes I do things that I later regret.
I usually think carefully before I do something.

I usually make decisions after careful and logical consideration.
For most decisions, it makes sense to rely on my intuition.
I am a very intuitive person.
The first idea is often the best.
When making purchasing decisions, I often go with my gut.
I find little satisfaction in thinking for hours on end.
Thinking abstractly does not appeal to me.
I would rather do something that requires little thinking than something that will certainly challenge my ability to think.
It is enough that something works, I don't care how or why.
I usually prefer to accept things as they are rather than question them.

Logical Thinking (Wechsler, 1958)

Q28. 1. all footballers are fit and healthy.
2. all famous athletes are soccer players.
Which of the following is the logical conclusion if the above statements are true?

All soccer players are famous athletes.
All famous people are fit and healthy. All famous athletes are fit and healthy.
All fit and healthy people are soccer players.

Q29. How many triangles are there in the 6th figure?

Q30. Which of the boxes below must the question mark be replaced with?

Q31. The grid is missing one box. Find out which of the boxes A to F completes the grid.

— Apostolakis, G., F. Kraanen, and G. van Dijk (2016): Examining pension beneficiaries' willingness to pay for a socially responsible and impact investment portfolio: A case study in the Dutch healthcare sector. *Journal of Behavioral and Experimental Finance, 11*, 27–43. https://doi.org/10.1016/J.JBEF.2016.06.001.
— Brunen, A. C. and O. Laubach (2021): Do sustainable consumers prefer socially responsible investments? A study among the users of robo advisors. *Journal of Banking & Finance*, 106314. https://doi.org/10.1016/J.JBANKFIN.2021.106314.
— Keller, J., G. Bohner, and H. P. Erb (2000): Intuitive and Heuristic Judgment – Different Processes? Presentation of a German Version of the Rational-Experiential Inventory and of New Self-Report Scales of Heuristic Use. *Zeitschrift Fur Sozialpsychologie, 31*(2), 87–101. https://doi.org/10.1024//0044-3514.31.2.87.
— Körner, A., M. Geyer, M. Roth, M. Drapeau, G. Schmutzer, C. Albani, S. Schumann, and E. Brähler (2008): Personality assessment with the NEO-Five-Factor Inventory: The 30-item-short-version (NEO-FFI-30). *PPmP Psychotherapie Psychosomatik Medizinische Psychologie, 58*(6), 238–245. https://doi.org/10.1055/S-2007-986199/ID/22.
— Kovaleva, A., C. Beierlein, C. J. Kemper, and B. Rammstedt (2012): *Eine Kurzskala zur Messung von Impulsivität nach dem UPPS-Ansatz : Die Skala Impulsives-Verhalten-8 (I-8)* (No. 20).

GESIS – Leibniz-Institut für Sozialwissenschaften. https://www.gesis.org/fileadmin/upload/forschung/publikationen/gesis_reihen/gesis_arbeitsberichte/WorkingPapers_2012-20.pdf.
— Lagerkvist, C. J., A. K. Edenbrandt, I. Tibbelin, and Y. Wahlstedt (2020): Preferences for sustainable and responsible equity funds – A choice experiment with Swedish private investors. *Journal of Behavioral and Experimental Finance, 28*, 100406. https://doi.org/10.1016/J.JBEF.2020.100406.
— Lusardi, A. and O. S. Mitchell (2014): The Economic Importance of Financial Literacy: Theory and Evidence. *Journal of Economic Literature, 52*(1), 5–44. https://doi.org/10.1257/JEL.52.1.5.
— Riebe, K. (2021): Determinants of Financial Literacy Among German Students – An Empirical Analysis. *Vierteljahrshefte Zur Wirtschaftsforschung, 89*(4), 39–54. https://doi.org/10.3790/VJH.89.4.39.
— Siemroth, C. and L. Hornuf (2021): *Do Retail Investors Value Environmental Impact? A Lab-in-the-Field Experiment with Crowdfunders.* www.RePEc.org.
— Wechsler, D. (1958). The Measurement and Appraisal of Adult Intelligence. In *The Measurement and Appraisal of Adult Intelligence* (4th ed.). Williams & Wilkins Co. https://doi.org/10.1037/11167-000.

Firms in Green Public Procurement: Financial Strength Indicators' Impact on Contract Awards and Its Repercussion on Financial Strength*, **

CHRISTOPHER F. BAUM, ARASH KORDESTANI, DOROTHEA SCHÄFER AND ANDREAS STEPHAN

Christopher F. Baum, Boston College, e-mail: baum@bc.edu
Arash Kordestani, Södertörn University, e-mail: arash.kordestani@sh.se
Dorothea Schäfer, DIW Berlin & Jönköping University, e-mail: dschaefer@diw.de
Andreas Stephan, Linnaeus University, e-mail: andreas.stephan@lnu.se

This work is part of the XPRESS project. This project has received funding from the European Union's Horizon 2020 Research and Innovation programme under Grant Agreement No. 857831, https://www.xpress-h2020.eu/.

Abstract: We examine whether the financial strength of companies, in particular, small and medium-sized enterprises (SMEs) is causally linked to the award of a public procurement contract (PP), especially in the environmentally friendly green area (GPP). For this purpose, we build a combined procurement company data set from the Tenders Electronic Daily (TED) and the SME database AMADEUS, which includes ten European countries. First, we apply probit models to investigate whether the probability of winning the public tender depends on the company's financial strength. We then use the flexpanel DiD approach to investigate the question of whether the award has an impact on the future financial strength of the successful company. On the

→ JEL classification: G30, Q56, Q01, O16
→ Keywords: Sustainable Finance, Public Procurement, Green Public Procurement, Small and Medium-sized Companies, Innovation, Financial constraints

* We are grateful to all cooperation partners in the XPRESS project, eAmbiente (ITA), University of York (UK), Element Energy (UK), Norwegian University of Science and Technology (NOR), Agenzia Per la Promozione della Ricerca Europea (ITA), Globaz Sa Loba (PT), International Network for SMEs (ITA), Research Centre for Energy Resources and Consumption (ESP), European Green Cities (DK), Alleanza per il Clima Italia (ITA), Climate Alliance Europe (DEU), Slovak Craft Industry Federation (SK) and European Association of Development Agencies (BE), for their help in identifying the successful companies in the Tenders Electronic Daily (TED) database that can be merged with AMADEUS. Special thanks go to Henriette Weser for her most valuable research assistance in constructing the data set during the first 20 months of the XPRESS project.

** Disclaimer: The information and views set out in this report are those of the author(s) and do not necessarily reflect the official opinion of the European Union. Neither the European Union institutions and bodies nor any person acting on their behalf may be held responsible for the use which may be made of the information contained herein.

one hand, we find that a lower equity ratio and a higher short-term debt ratio increase the probability of being successful in a public tender. On the other hand, a success means that the companies can continue to work after the award with a lower equity ratio than comparable companies without an award, regardless of whether the company was successful in a traditional or a green public tender. We conclude from this that the success in a PP is a substitute for a firm's own financial strength and thus facilitates access to external financing.

Zusammenfassung: Wir untersuchen, ob die Finanzkraft von Unternehmen, insbesondere Klein- und Mittelständischen Unternehmen (KMU), kausal mit dem Zuschlag für einen öffentlichen Auftrag (PP), insbesondere im umweltfreundlichen Bereich verbunden ist. Hierzu konstruieren wir aus der Tenders Electronic Daily (TED) und der KMU-Datenbank AMADEUS einen kombinierten Beschaffungs-Unternehmen-Datensatz, der zehn europäische Länder umfasst. Zunächst prüfen wir mit Hilfe von Probit-Modellen, ob die Wahrscheinlichkeit des Zuschlags bei der öffentlichen Ausschreibung von der Finanzkraft des Unternehmens abhängt. Anschließend nutzen wir den Flexpanel-DiD-Ansatz, um der Frage nachzugehen, ob der Zuschlag auf die zukünftige Finanzkraft des erfolgreichen Unternehmens zurückwirkt. Wir finden einerseits, dass eine niedrigere Eigenkapitalquote und eine höhere Quote kurzfristiger Kredite die Wahrscheinlichkeit erhöhen, bei einer öffentlichen Ausschreibung, sei sie traditionell oder „grüner" Natur, erfolgreich zu sein. Andererseits bewirkt der Erfolg, dass die erfolgreichen Unternehmen nach dem Zuschlag mit einer geringeren Eigenkapitalquote weiterarbeiten können als vergleichbare Unternehmen ohne Zuschlag, unabhängig davon, ob das Unternehmen in einer traditionellen oder einer „grünen" öffentlichen Ausschreibung erfolgreich war. Wir schließen daraus, dass der Zuschlag ein Substitut für eigene Finanzstärke ist und dadurch den Zugang zu Fremdfinanzierung erleichtert.

Introduction

From 2015 to 2017 numerous EU public authorities spent approximately 2 trillion Euros annually, around 14% of GDP, on the purchase of services, works and supplies (European Commission 2019). Although Green Public Procurement (GPP) has been a small share of this total expenditure, it is expected to grow considerably in the coming years. According to the EU Commission, Green Public Procurement is "a process whereby public authorities seek to procure goods, services and works with a reduced environmental impact throughout their life cycle when compared to goods, services and works with the same primary function that would otherwise be procured" (COM 2008, p. 400 "Public procurement for a better environment"). By launching so-called green tenders and awarding offers for goods, services, and works that protect the environment more effectively than conventional variants, public authorities' purchasing power contributes to the Great Green Transition (Kemfert, Schäfer and Semmler 2020). Firms that compete for the green procurement contracts and financial institutions that fund the applicants are the mediators in this process.

In this paper, we shed new light on how public procurement (PP) in general and GPP in particular are linked to the applicants' financial strength. Specifically, we use the Tenders Electronic Daily (TED) database of the European Union to identify those firms that were successful in receiving PPs and GPPs. Using TED and the AMADEUS firm database we build a dataset of successful procurement firms and peers that qualify as suit control group. First, we apply a Probit panel data model to investigate how the firm's financial strength affects the likelihood of winning a public procurement tender. Second, we capture the causal effect of the Green Public Procurement success on financial strength by employing the flexpanel DiD approach (Dettmann, Giebler and Weyh 2020).

We establish two main results. On the one hand, we find that a lower equity ratio and a higher ratio of short-term credits increase the likelihood of being successful in a public tender, be the tender of a general or green nature. On the other hand, we find that successful companies can continue to operate after the success with a lower equity ratio than comparable companies without such a success.

Our research is closely related to the literature exploring the impact of public procurement on firms' financial barriers and on innovation. However, we note that there is a blind spot in research regarding traditional public procurements and there is literally no research considering the link between green public procurement and a firm's financial strength neither for firms in general nor for SMEs in particular. To the best of our knowledge we are the first to address these issues.

The rest of the paper proceeds as follows. The next Section gives an overview of the related research. Then, we describe the dataset. We procede with the empirical approach and the estimation results. The final Section concludes.

Previous Research

Investment in technologies to achieve a low carbon economy produces positive externalities in both the innovation and diffusion stages. This causes market failure and underinvestment, as the private returns from those investments are lower than the social returns (Rennings 2000, Kemp and Oltra 2011, De Marchi 2012). The discrepancy between private and social returns justifies policy intervention. Public procurement is a particular type of policy intervention. It is considered to be a key policy instrument, not only to incentivize private actors to broaden the application of existing Renewable Energy Supply (RES) technologies, but also to develop innovative RES products and solutions. Public Procurement is not direct public funding, but rather an instrument to allocate and distribute public funds in return for societal benefits.

The issue of funding innovations in renewable energy supply (RES) is of growing interest both for firms and policy makers as RES innovations pave the way to a low carbon economy. Currently, little is known about how SMEs finance the purchase of new clean energy and technologies necessary to make production processes and distribution channels climate-friendly, and what restrictions SMEs face vìs-à-vìs large firms in financing RES innovations. In general, the funding possibilities of RES innovators, be they on the forefront in applying innovative RES technologies or in creating new climate-tech solutions, are constrained. Environmental innovation projects are long-term commitments often associated with immature and complex technologies (Olmos, Ruester and Liong 2012). The long payback period reinforces the perceived risk of such investments (Ghisetti, Mancinelli, Mazzanti and Zoli 2017). In addition, innovative firms often own large stocks of intangible assets that cannot be pledged as collateral (Brown, Martinsson and Petersen 2012, Cosci, Meliciani and Sabato 2016, Hall, Moncada-Paternò-Castello, Montresor and Vezzani 2016).

Although opaqueness and information asymmetry between borrowers and investors are particularly problematic for SMEs, those obstacles are even more pervasive for environmental innovation projects (Cecere, Corrocher, Gossart and Ozman 2014a, Jensen, Schäfer and Stephan 2019). Accordingly, immaturity of some RES markets, a greater perceived risk of the investment in environmental innovations (Aghion, Veugelers and Hemous 2009, Ghisetti et al. 2017), fierce competition from fossil-fuel-affine incumbents and an insufficient recognition of climate risks in rating models, including the banks' own internal models, work in favor of funding constraints and often induce financial institutions to shy away from supplying the required funds (Hottenrott and Peters 2012, Schäfer, Stephan and Mosquera 2017).

Public procurement has the potential to stimulate firms' innovation (Appelt and Galindo-Rueda 2016, Aschhoff and Sofka 2009, Czarnitzki, Hünermund and Moshgbar 2018). Success in public procurement tenders also has a crucial role in improving innovation success, measured in terms of turnover achieved with new products (Ghisetti 2017). Czarnitzki et al. (2018) study the effect of changes in innovation policy enforced in 2009 on turnover changes in three years after 2009. They find that turnover with new products and services benefits from public procurement of innovations. Also, a study on US firms shows the positive effect of awarding a tender on stock returns of the firms (Larson and Picou 2002).

Cheng, Appolloni, D'Amato and Zhu (2018) study Green Public Procurement (GPP). They see the main benefits of GPP as its ability to be a demand-pull factor and "market trigger," meaning that GPP is able to enlarge the market for environmentally friendly goods and services. However, the authors also point out that there has been inadequate attention given in the academic literature to the impact of GPP. Zipperer (2019) provides evidence on the relationship between GPP and firms' innovation activities. Her findings confirm the demand-pull effect of GPP for general product innovations, but not specifically for environmental innovations. Czarnitzki, Hünermund and Moshgbar (2018) find a robust and significant effect of innovation-directed public procurement on turnover from new products and services. However, the effect seems to be restricted to innovations of a more incremental nature instead of market novelties. Cecere, Corrocher, Gossart and Ozman (2014b) propose that access to public funds and fiscal incentives contribute to improve firms' ability to introduce eco-innovations as firms consider public funding to be complementary to other external finance.

The question of how public procurement is linked to a firm's financial strength has received little attention in both corporate finance and innovation research. This is surprising. A firm's financial strength may influence their success in a public procurement tender. In addition, winning a procurement contract may influence the successful firm's financial strength and, via this channel, their access to future funding. There is clearly a blind spot in research regarding traditional public procurement tenders but there is literally no research considering the link between green public procurement and a firm's financial strength for firms, either in general or for SMEs in particular. The pecking order theory claims that internal financial strength is key for a firm's capability to invest (Myers and Majluf 1984). Participating in a public tender is an investment from the firm's point of view. The size of the investment might shape the firm's chances to win. In addition, the public authorities launching the tender and deciding which firm gets the award might be particularly concerned that the firms has the means to carry out the investments necessary to finish the project successfully. On the other hand, young and growing firms may make particularly high investments to increase the chances of winning the tender. Rapidly growing firms may lack high equity ratios and may rely on short-term debt and trade credit. Accordingly, the question arises whether the firm's financial strength affects the chance to win a tender in a public procurement.

Hottenrott and Peters (2012) argue that the access to external finance depends on firms' creditworthiness. The invitation to tender for goods and services commonly implies that the award winners gain substantial additional demand in markets. If these products are new, little-tested goods and services, the award supports building a market that has not yet been established. This effect is known as the demand-pull effect of public procurement. On the one hand, this demand provides companies with the necessary incentives to invest in product improvement and marketability, and on the other hand, it also is an instrument for de-risking the financial institutions' financial claims and increasing the award winner's creditworthiness. From this perspective, Public Procurement (PP) is an important instrument for strengthening the financial institution's willingness to fund the firm. In other words, PP can be an essential tool for easing the funding constraints of companies which can pave the way to a green economy. However, empirically, whether gaining a contract award contributes positively to the creditworthiness of innovators is still an open question.

We address these important issues using a self-constructed dataset that combines financial firm-level data and public procurement data. The particular strength of our dataset is the possibility to exploit the heterogeneity of firms across different dimensions of interest, overall vs. green public procurement specifically and firms in general and SMEs in particular.

Causal inferences have paramount importance in econometric research to estimate the effect of policies (Hünermund and Czarnitzki, 2019). There are several biases in estimating causal effects in policy research including but not limited to sample selection, and confounding effects (Bareinboim and Pearl 2016). As Hünermund and Czarnitzki (2019) discuss for firms that receive R&D grants, there are several screenings before a firm can receive a R&D grant, involving both observable and unobservable firm characteristics. As a result, a naive sample containing funded and unfunded firms would fail to consider confounding variables. Hence, it is recommended to consider confounding variables as much as possible by collaboration with funding organizations and including financial variables (Hünermund and Czarnitzki, 2019). In this study, we use key financial and size variables to create reliable groups of treatment and control firms.

Data

The Tenders Electronic Daily (TED) database and the AMADEUS firm database are the two sources on which we base our assessment. TED is the public procurement database of the European Union, containing Contract Award Notices (CAN). It "publishes 746 thousand procurement [contract] award notices a year, including 235 thousand calls for tenders which are worth approximately € 545 billion."[1] Calls for tenders are invitations to bid for a project. Public tenders are those in which governments and other public authorities such as cities and communities invite enterprises to bid for projects. The invitation is a formal procurement document issued by the buyer specifying the terms, which the potential suppliers must meet in order to submit an acceptable bid.

The TED database only contains details of those firms, which have submitted a successful bid, as documented in a CAN. Those firms are the Contract Award (CA) firms. All information obtained from the CAN is available at the firm level. In 2014, the European Union implemented a Public Procurement policy reform aimed at enhancing SME participation. The key feature was that large contracts could be broken up into smaller lots. Those smaller lots should enable SMEs to submit a tender for a lot instead of the total contract value. The CAN data in the estimation sample range from 2015–2018 (post-SME reform period) and cover ten European countries: Belgium (BE),

1 https://ted.europa.eu/TED/main/HomePage.do.

Denmark (DK), Germany (DE), Great Britain (GB), Italy (IT), Norway (NO), Portugal (PT), Slovakia (SK), Spain (ES) and Sweden (SE).[2]

To produce causal inference on the two questions of how a firm's financial strength affects the likelihood to be a successful bidder and how success influences the bidder's financial strength afterwards, CA firms must be compared with appropriate control firms. Bidding firms that failed to receive a CA would be the ideal candidates for the control group of successful CA firms, but data on the unsuccessful bidders is not available in the TED database. Thus, we apply an alternative strategy to establish a suitable control group, making use of AMADEUS, a database of European SMEs compiled by BvD. AMADEUS contains financial data from the companies' balance sheet and income statements. We select companies with yearly financial and employment data in the period 2010–2019 from their unconsolidated accounts. As AMADEUS reports financial data in domestic currencies, we apply the official Euro foreign exchange reference rates (ECB) to obtain Euro (EUR) values. We retain only those AMADEUS firms that are in the same industries as the CA firms from the TED database.

Table 1

Number of observations for Contract Award (CA) firms and control firms

	Firm-years	Percent	Cumulative Percent
noTED	**5952**	48.50	48.50
TED	**6325**	51.50	100.00
Total	**12277**	100.00	.

Source: TED and AMADEUS, own calculations.

In the first step of building the sample of treated and control firms, we merge the CA firms from TED with financial and employment data from AMADEUS. The merging assigns key information to each CA firm for the years prior to success, in the year of success and the following years. In the second step, we apply a matching technique to select control firms from the AMADEUS database to be added to the CA firms. The matched firms did not receive a CA, but are similar to the successful firms in year (t-1) prior to the CA in key indicators: the equity ratio, total assets, and employment. Their similarity one year before the CA year is crucial, as it supports identifying the causal effect of the CA on the successful firms' financial strength.

The entire sample of treated CA firms and non-treated control firms consists of 12277 firm-years in total. 6325 firm-years belong to Contract Award (CA) firms from the TED dataset, and 5952 firm-years are observed in the group of control firms taken from the AMADEUS database. In total, between 2015 and 2018 we observe 1022 firms that have received a CA in one of 10 EU countries. The number of firms varies significantly across the 10 countries under consideration. For example, the final sample contains 226 CA firms from Great Britain but only 45 CA firms in Denmark. In an ideal setting the number of observations (firm-years in total) would equal the number of firms times the number of observed years. However, the complete range of years is often not observed.

2 The XPRESS project focuses on these countries.

Thus, the panel is unbalanced, and the shares in firm-numbers and firm-years deviate from each other for the total of all 10 countries as well as for single countries.

The CA firms are almost evenly distributed over this period as Table 2 below shows. The highest frequency of CA incidences is observed in the year 2017 but the differences in the frequencies across years are rather small.

Table 2

Distribution of successful firms over years of observation

Year	Number of firms	Percent	Cumulative Percent
2015	**218**	21.26	21.26
2016	**242**	23.72	44.98
2017	**284**	27.95	72.93
2018	**278**	27.07	100.00
Total	**1022**	100.00	

Source: TED and AMADEUS, own calculations.

The Common Procurement Vocabulary (CPV) allows us to identify tenders from the area of Green Public Procurement (GPP). Table 3 below shows the CPVs of GPP tenders (see the different tender types in more detail in the Appendix). We label the successful suppliers of goods, services and works as green companies. The sample contains 1237 observations for green companies. The green CA firms are most frequently active in the areas "Electricity, heating, solar and nuclear energy", "Electric vehicles", "Wood fuels" and "Heat pumps". The least number of firm-years are observed in the areas of "Solar collectors for heat production" and "Wind farms".

Table 3

Green CA firms

CPV: CA in Green Public Procurements (GPP)	Firm-years	Percent	Cumulative Percent
Fuel wood	**9**	0.73	0.73
Wood waste	**19**	1.54	2.26
Wood fuels	**107**	8.65	10.91
Biodiesel	**10**	0.81	11.72
Electricity, heating, solar and nuclear energy	**263**	21.26	32.98
Solar energy	**57**	4.61	37.59
Solar panels	**46**	3.72	41.31
Solar collectors for heat production	**5**	0.40	41.71
Solar photovoltaic modules	**48**	3.88	45.59
Solar installation	**42**	3.40	48.99
Wind energy generators	**36**	2.91	51.90
Wind turbines	**10**	0.81	52.71
Wind farm	**5**	0.40	53.11
Semiconductors	**10**	0.81	53.92
Electric vehicles	**255**	20.61	74.54

Table 3 *(Continued)*

CPV: CA in Green Public Procurements (GPP)	Firm-years	Percent	Cumulative Percent
Electric buses	35	2.83	77.36
Heat pumps	96	7.76	85.13
Hydro-electric plant construction work	77	6.22	91.35
Thermal power plant construction	30	2.43	93.78
Wind-power installation works	26	2.10	95.88
Roof-covering work	51	4.12	100.00
Total	1237	100.00	

Source: TED and AMADEUS, own calculations.

In addition, we identify tenders that may or may not belong to the area of GPP (see Appendix 1). We label those suppliers as "green possible" firms. Those firms are most frequently active in the areas "Petroleum products, fuel, electricity and other sources of energy", "Electricity", "Energy and related services" and "Electricity distribution and control apparatus".

Unfortunately, we cannot uniquely infer from the CPV codes whether "green possible" tenders definitely belong to the GPP segment. Clearly labeling such tenders either as compatible or incompatible with the EU Green Deal and, thus, GPP goods, services and works would avoid any ambiguity and support incentivizing green innovation. Many governments intend to increase their issuances of "green sovereign bonds". Of course, money in itself is not green, and so the proceeds from those issuances are not in itself green. Those bonds can only be advertised as green if the proceeds from the issuance are used to finance investments in green projects or purchases of green goods and services. Therefore, an easier identification of those tenders that qualify for public promotion and, thus, can be financed by issuing sovereign green bonds would most likely support the development of a strong and highly liquid market for sovereign green bonds (Wulandari, Schäfer, Stephan and Sun 2018). In addition, easy identification facilitates better auditing and supports the prevention of "greenwashing".

Finally, for reasons of completeness, we identify the tenders that certainly do not deserve the green label. We name the respective CA firms as brown firms (see Appendix 1). The brown firms are most frequently active in the areas "Refuse incineration services", "District-heating mains construction work" and "District-heating plant construction work".

Empirical Approach

The following sections present the multivariate analysis of CA firms vis-à-vis the control firms. As a first step, we construct key financial ratios that are appropriate to indicate financial strength. We consider the equity ratio, the long-term debt ratio, the short-term debt ratio, the loan ratio, the trade credit ratio and the turnover ratio. Those indicators of financial strength are expressed as a percentage of total assets.

Table 4

Financial strength and size indicators

Variable	Description
	Financial strength indicators
Equity ratio	Shareholder funds (equity) divided by total assets
LTDB ratio	Noncurrent liabilities: long-term debt (LTDB) to total assets
STDB ratio	Short-term debt ratio: sum of loan and credits divided by total assets
LOAN ratio	Loan divided by total assets
CRED ratio	Trade credit divided by total assets
TURN ratio	Turnover divided by total assets
	Size indicators
Log (Total Assets)	Logarithmic transformation of total assets
SME/nonSME	SME if the firm has less than 250 employees, non SME otherwise

Source: AMADEUS, own calculations. The Equity ratio is winsorized at the 1th percentiles. Log (Total Assets) is winsorized at 1th and 99th percentiles.

We first hypothesize:

H1: The likelihood of winning a public procurement tender depends on the firm's financial strength.

To test this hypothesis, we use a probit model with the dependent variable *TEDyear* and firm characteristics as independent regressors. *TEDyear* takes on the value of one in the year the firm wins the TED contract award and zero otherwise. The main variable of interest is the indicator of the firm's financial strength. The control variables are the log of total assets, a dummy indicating being an SME, year dummies from 2015 to 2018, industry and country dummies. We use the EU standard definition of a SME as any firm with fewer than 250 employees.

We consider four subsamples as defined in Table 5. The most interesting ones are the subsamples of all firms, which received a CA in a GPP tender and their non-treated control firms (3), and the subsample of all SMEs which received a CA in a GPP tender and their non-treated control SMEs (4).

Table 5

Definition of the indicator variable TEDyear depending on the subsample under consideration

Dependent Variable (Sample)	Sample description
TEDyear (1)	= 1 if the firm wins any tender, zero otherwise (Overall sample: **All firms** which received a CA and control firms)
TEDyear (2)	Among SMEs: = 1 if the SME wins any tender, zero otherwise (Subsample: **All SMEs** which received a CA and control SMEs)
TEDyear (3)	Among firms winning a green public procurement (GPP CA): = 1 if the firm wins a tender, zero otherwise (Subsample: **All firms** which received a **GPP CA** and control firms)
TEDyear (4)	Among SMEs winning a green public procurement (GPP CA): = 1 if the firm wins a tender, zero otherwise (Subsample: **All SMEs** which received a **GPP CA** and control SMEs)

In the second step, we hypothesize:

H2: Winning a tender has an impact on the firm's financial strength in the years after the contract award.

To explore this hypothesis, we apply the flexpanel difference-in-difference approach (DiD) (Dettmann et al. 2020) to similar subsamples as those defined in Table 5. The DiD approach reveals whether firms with a CA (treatment group) develop differently in the years after winning the contract award than the similar firms without a CA (control group). In order to create the treatment and control groups, we construct a dummy variable called *treated* with values 1 if the company has won a public procurement contract between year 2015 and 2018 (treatment group) and zero otherwise (control group). Then, to capture the period effect that applies to both treated and non-treated firms, we create another dummy called *Posttreatment period*. This variable takes on the value of one starting from year *t+1* where t is the year of success. Our main variable of interest is the *Treatment effect*. This dummy variable represents the interaction between the variables *treated* and *Posttreatment period*. The *Treatment effect* is zero if, and only if, the dummy variable *treated* is zero. It is 1 if the dummies *Posttreatment period* and *treated* are 1. Table 6 describes the main treatment variables used in flexpanel DiD regression equation.

Table 6

Treatment effect

Treatment effect	Dummy variable	Values
Winning a tender	treated	0: no win; 1: winning at least one contract award (CA) in 2015 and 2018
Period effect for both the treated and the non-treated firm(s)	Posttreatment period	0 for treatment and matched control firm before the contract award (CA) success; 1 for both firm types one year after winning a tender, and then it repeats afterwards. A maximum of three years after winning a tender between 2015 and 2018 is considered.
Interaction between winning a tender and post treatment effect	Treatment effect (treated # Posttreatment period)	0: no effect; 1: effect Full interaction effect between winning a contract award and the period after the treatment

Previous studies propose various control variables. Aschhoff and Sofka (2009) include control variables capturing market innovation. Fazekas and Tóth (2017) use country labels and indicators of market level interventions. Ghisetti (2017) adds control variables for environmental innovation. The TED dataset provides a variety of candidates for control variables. We abstain from incorporating a multitude of control variables to keep the model as simple as possible. We use total assets, country, firm type, NACE codes and time dummies for the years between 2011 and 2018 as control variables in the flexpanel DiD models.

Does Financial Strength Affect the Likelihood of Winning a Tender?

We start with the first question of whether the likelihood of winning a public procurement tender is associated with a higher financial strength. Table 7 shows the descriptive statistics of the financial strength indicators of interest separately for TED firms and the noTED companies in the overall Sample (1). The Table reveals that the CA firms in the estimation samples have on average a lower equity ratio, a higher short-term debt ratio, a higher trade credit ratio and a higher turnover ratio.

Table 7

Descriptive statistics of financial ratios and size indicators for TED and noTED firms in the overall sample (1)

Variable	Obs.	Mean	Q1	Median	Q3	Min	Max	STD
				TED firms				
Equity ratio	2748	0.33***	0.15	0.32	0.49	0.00	1.00	0.23
LTDB ratio	2367	0.11	0.00	0.02	0.16	0.00	1.00	0.17
STDB ratio	2646	0.25***	0.07	0.19	0.38	0.00	1.00	0.23
LOAN ratio	2663	0.09**	0.00	0.01	0.11	0.00	1.00	0.15
CRED ratio	2686	0.17***	0.03	0.11	0.25	0.00	1.00	0.18
TURN ratio	1962	2.22*	0.76	1.25	2.43	0.00	840.40	19.03
Log (Total Assets)	1973	17.38***	15.73	17.63	18.90	10.91	23.00	2.32
SME	1973	0.74	0.00	1.00	1.00	0.00	1.00	0.44
Variable				noTED firms				
Equity ratio	2593	0.38	0.15	0.36	0.56	0.00	1.00	0.26
LTDB ratio	2224	0.11	0.00	0.01	0.16	0.00	1.00	0.19
STDB ratio	2480	0.21	0.04	0.15	0.32	0.00	1.00	0.22
LOAN ratio	2499	0.08	0.00	0.01	0.09	0.00	1.00	0.14
CRED ratio	2510	0.14	0.02	0.08	0.19	0.00	1.00	0.16
TURN ratio	1788	1.42	0.53	1.07	1.88	0.00	21.62	1.42
Log (Total Assets)	1797	17.15	15.48	17.44	18.61	11.23	23.00	2.29
SME	1797	0.76	1.00	1.00	1.00	0.00	1.00	0.43

Source: AMADEUS, own calculations. The Equity ratio is winsorized at the 1th percentiles. The other variables including the Log (Total Assets) are winsorized at 1th and 99th percentiles. The descriptive statistics are obtained from the estimation sample of the Probit regression on the overall sample (1). The regression employs the lagged versions of either the Equity ratio, LTDB ratio, STDB ratio, LOAN ratio, CRED ratio or TURN ratio as independent variable. The descriptive statistics for the control variables Log (Total Assets) and the dummy variable SME are obtained from the Probit regression in which the lagged TURN ratio is the independent variable. T-tests on the difference of means of TED and non-TED firms. *** significant at 1 %, ** significant at 5 %, * significant at 10 %.

Table 8 shows the descriptive statistics for Sample (3), the sample of successful firms in Green Public Procurements (TED firms) and their control firms (noTED firms). The Table shows that the CA firms in the estimation sample have on average a lower equity ratio, a higher short-term debt ratio, a higher trade credit ratio and a higher turnover ratio.

Table 8

Descriptive statistics of financial ratios and size indicators for TED and noTED firms in the sample of successful firms in Green Public Procurements and their control firms

Variable	Obs.	Mean	Q1	Median	Q3	Min	Max	STD
				TED firms				
Equity ratio	460	0.31 ***	0.12	0.27	0.46	0.00	0.99	0.23
LTDB ratio	411	0.10	0.00	0.01	0.10	0.00	1.00	0.18
STDB ratio	443	0.27 ***	0.08	0.22	0.42	0.00	1.00	0.23
LOAN ratio	443	0.09	0.00	0.01	0.15	0.00	0.71	0.15
CRED ratio	448	0.18 ***	0.04	0.12	0.27	0.00	1.00	0.18

Table 8 *(Continued)*

Variable	Obs.	Mean	Q1	Median	Q3	Min	Max	STD
				TED firms				
TURN ratio	344	1.57	0.58	1.15	2.10	0.00	16.90	1.55
Log (Total Assets)	345	16.74 **	15.00	16.70	18.63	10.91	21.45	2.35
SME	345	0.78	1.00	1.00	1.00	0.00	1.00	0.41
Variable				**noTED firms**				
Equity ratio	2367	0.37	0.14	0.35	0.56	0.00	1.00	0.26
LTDB ratio	2017	0.11	0.00	0.01	0.13	0.00	1.00	0.18
STDB ratio	2274	0.22	0.04	0.16	0.33	0.00	1.00	0.22
LOAN ratio	2289	0.08	0.00	0.00	0.10	0.00	1.00	0.14
CRED ratio	2303	0.14	0.02	0.09	0.20	0.00	1.00	0.17
TURN ratio	1614	1.45	0.50	1.11	1.96	0.00	21.62	1.44
Log (Total Assets)	1621	17.05	15.35	17.24	18.58	11.23	23.00	2.34
SME	1621	0.76	1.00	1.00	1.00	0.00	1.00	0.43

Source: See notes in Table 7.

The following Tables 9–13 show the Average Marginal Effects (AME) of the probit regressions. The first probit regression models in Table 9 assess whether the probability of CA success depends on the *Equity ratio* before the year of winning the CA. Columns (1) and (2) report the coefficients for the overall sample vis-à-vis SMEs. Columns (3) and (4) show the estimation results for GPP contracts. Across all specifications, we find a significantly negative effect of the equity ratio (one year before the contract award) on the chance to win a CA. Firms with high equity ratios are less likely to receive a CA. A possible explanation for this result could be that companies which have a high debt ratio are in their expanding phase. Such companies are more likely to participate in the public procurement market and to put more effort and resources into winning tenders than settled firms with higher equity ratios. The negative effect of the equity ratio on the CA success probability is even stronger for SMEs. The strongest negative effect is obtained in the subsample of SMEs receiving a GPP tender. Equity-poor SMEs bidding in a green tender may have even higher incentives than large firms to overcome their constraints and to be successful. In this case, the low equity ratio indicates high constraints but also high incentives to overcome these constraints, and, thus, works as an advantage rather than a disadvantage.

Table 9

Likelihood of winning a contract award (prob TEDyear) depending on the lagged Equity ratio

TEDyear	(1) All firms	(2) All SMEs	(3) All firms with GPP CA	(4) All SMEs with GPP CA
Equity ratio (t-1)	-0.0889***	-0.0995***	-0.0375**	-0.0569***
	(-3.33)	(-3.49)	(-2.29)	(-2.90)
log(Total Assets)	0.0183***	0.0115***	0.00118	-0.000823
	(5.76)	(3.07)	(0.66)	(-0.35)
SME	0.0301**		0.0218**	
	(1.97)		(2.40)	

Table 9 *(Continued)*

TEDyear	(1) All firms	(2) All SMEs	(3) All firms with GPP CA	(4) All SMEs with GPP CA
lnsig2u	-1.442***	-2.017***	-2.673**	-2.498**
	(-7.44)	(-5.89)	(-2.26)	(-2.12)
Year Dummies (2015-2018)	YES	YES	YES	YES
Country Dummies	YES	YES	YES	YES
Industry Dummies	YES	YES	YES	YES
N	5341	3865	2827	2072
# Firms	1382	1060	729	570

Average marginal effects. t statistics in parentheses, $*p < 0.10$, $**p < 0.05$, $***p < 0.01$

Firm size has a significant effect on winning a tender in the overall sample and the SME sample. However, firm size is insignificant in the subsamples in which the treated firms received a green tender (GPP CA). In other words, size seems to be an important determinant of success in traditional but not in green tenders. *SMEs* have a higher chance of winning compared to non-*SMEs*.

Table 10 reports the findings with respect to the role of the short-term debt ratio for winning a CA. We also investigated the importance of the long-term debt *(LTDB) ratio* for the chance of receiving a CA. However, we obtained insignificant results across all samples. In contrast, the *STDB ratio* appears to have an impact. The effect is positive and significant only in the overall and in the SME sample. The significant coefficients show that companies which have a higher combination of short-term borrowing and trade credits (relative to their balance sheet amounts) are more likely to win tenders. In other words, firms which are in the expansion phase and use heavily trade credits and loans to grow the company are more likely to be successful. Importantly, this effect does not come through in GPP tenders. Within this segment, the *STDB ratio* does not significantly affect the firms' chance of winning a CA.

Table 10

Likelihood of winning a contract award (prob TEDyear) depending on the lagged STDB ratio

TEDyear	(1) All firms	(2) All SMEs	(3) All firms with GPP CA	(4) All SMEs with GPP CA
STDB ratio (t-1)	0.0873***	0.0803**	0.0251	0.0192
	(2.96)	(2.53)	(1.49)	(0.90)
log(Total Assets)	0.0180***	0.0112***	0.00168	-0.0000738
	(5.49)	(2.84)	(0.89)	(-0.03)
SME	0.0268*		0.0213**	
	(1.71)		(2.29)	
lnsig2u	-1.409***	-1.902***	-2.621**	-2.386**
	(-7.22)	(-5.87)	(-2.31)	(-2.21)
Year Dummies (2015-2018)	YES	YES	YES	YES
Country Dummies	YES	YES	YES	YES

Table 10 *(Continued)*

TEDyear	(1) All firms	(2) All SMEs	(3) All firms with GPP CA	(4) All SMEs with GPP CA
Industry Dummies	YES	YES	YES	YES
N	5192	3748	2756	2012
# Firms	1366	1044	721	560

Average marginal effects. t statistics in parentheses, p < 0.10, ** p < 0.05, *** p < 0.01

Disentangling the joint effect of the *STDB ratio* into a separate loan and trade credit effect provides a clearer picture of the drivers of these results. The *LOAN ratio* in Table 11 shows a significantly positive coefficient in the overall sample of firms. In other words, in principle, the higher is the loan share in the company's balance sheet, the greater is their chance of winning a tender. However, the *LOAN ratio* has no effect for SME success, nor does it affect the chances of winning a GPP. Total assets are again a decisive factor for winning a tender, but not in the samples of GPP tenders. *SMEs* are advantaged in winning tenders compared to bigger companies.

Table 11

Likelihood of winning a contract award (prob TEDyear) depending on the lagged LOAN ratio

TEDyear	(1) All firms	(2) All SMEs	(3) All firms with GPP CA	(4) All SMEs with GPP CA
LOAN ratio (t-1)	0.0916**	0.0693	0.00815	0.00851
	(2.14)	(1.44)	(0.31)	(0.27)
log(Total Assets)	0.0179***	0.0112***	0.00173	-0.000104
	(5.51)	(2.86)	(0.93)	(-0.04)
SME	0.0276*		0.0215**	
	(1.77)		(2.32)	
lnsig2u	-1.394***	-1.875***	-2.480**	-2.281**
	(-7.24)	(-5.94)	(-2.48)	(-2.31)
Year Dummies	YES	YES	YES	YES
Country Dummies	YES	YES	YES	YES
Industry Dummies	YES	YES	YES	YES
N	5214	3770	2763	2019
# Firms	1366	1044	721	560

Average marginal effects. t statistics in parentheses, * p < 0.10, ** p < 0.05, *** p < 0.01

The *CRED ratio* effects reveal that only this particular type of short-term debt affects the chance of winning a CA in a GPP (Table 12). The coefficients are not only positive and significant in the overall and in the SME sample, but also in the overall sample of all firms covering GPP. A high share of trade credits increases the chance of winning in a GPP. A higher share of trade credits is an even stronger indication of rapidly expanding firms with high financing needs than a high share of short-term loans. Such rapidly expanding firms have a higher chance of success also in GPP tenders. The effect of the total assets variable is restricted to the All firms and All SMEs samples. *SMEs* are advantaged in winning tenders compared to bigger companies.

Table 12

Likelihood of winning a contract award (prob TEDyear) depending on the lagged CRED ratio

TEDyear	(1) All firms	(2) All SMEs	(3) All firms with GPP CA	(4) All SMEs with GPP CA
CRED ratio (t-1)	0.0871**	0.102**	0.0392*	0.0301
	(2.20)	(2.43)	(1.67)	(1.03)
log(Total Assets)	0.0185***	0.0112***	0.00149	-0.000560
	(5.66)	(2.85)	(0.79)	(-0.22)
SME	0.0274*		0.0221**	
	(1.76)		(2.42)	
lnsig2u	-1.388***	-1.922***	-2.787**	-2.524**
	(-7.29)	(-5.88)	(-2.17)	(-2.13)
Time Dummies	YES	YES	YES	YES
Country Dummies	YES	YES	YES	YES
Industry Dummies	YES	YES	YES	YES
N	5235	3768	2773	2023
# Firms	1371	1048	722	562

Average marginal effects. *t* statistics in parentheses, $^{*}p < 0.10$, $^{**}p < 0.05$, $^{***}p < 0.01$

The turnover ratio (*TURN ratio*) has no significant impact on winning a tender (Table 13). This finding is in line with the notion that expanding firms are more likely to win a tender, but less so firms, which are already settled in terms of equity and turnover. Overall, our findings partially confirm Hypothesis 1. The *Equity ratio* lowers the chance of winning a CA in tradition PP and even more so in GPP. A high short-term debt share increases the likelihood of success for firms and SMEs in general but not for green firms. In GPP, only a high share of trade credits vis-à-vis the control firms has that effect.

Table 13

Likelihood of winning a contract award (prob TEDyear) depending on the lagged TURN ratio

TEDyear	(1) All firms	(2) All SMEs	(3) All firms with GPP CA	(4) All SMEs with GPP CA
TURN ratio (t-1)	-0.000241	-0.000246	0.00169	0.00212
	(-0.91)	(-1.00)	(0.61)	(0.68)
log(Total Assets)	0.0169***	0.0143***	0.00147	0.00101
	(4.14)	(3.15)	(0.61)	(0.34)
SME	0.00240		0.0183	
	(0.12)		(1.56)	
lnsig2u	-1.301***	-1.692***	-11.44	-14.70
	(-6.08)	(-5.27)	(-0.00)	(-0.00)
Year Dummies	YES	YES	YES	YES
Country Dummies	YES	YES	YES	YES
Industry Dummies	YES	YES	YES	YES
N	3770	2836	1966	1502

Table 13 *(Continued)*

TEDyear	(1) All firms	(2) All SMEs	(3) All firms with GPP CA	(4) All SMEs with GPP CA
# Firms	980	756	509	400

Average marginal effects. *t* statistics in parentheses, * $p < 0.10$, ** $p < 0.05$, *** $p < 0.01$

Does Winning a Public Procurement Tender Promote a Firm's Financial Strength?

In this section, we turn to testing Hypothesis 2. We fit DiD models to assess the impact of winning a CA in a public procurement on a firm's future financial strength. Our focus is on the *Equity ratio* and the *STDB ratio* as the two indicators that were found to have a significant impact on the chance of winning a tender.

Table 14 reports the DiD results for the *Equity ratio*. The *Treatment effect* is significantly negative in the samples of All firms and All Firms with GPP CA. The success lowers the firms' equity ratio over the next years no matter whether the success is in a general PP or a GPP tender. In contrast, the coefficients of the *Treatment effect* of SMEs remain insignificant. SMEs with lower equity ratios have a higher chance to be successful in a tender, but after the success the equity ratios of SMEs in treatment and control group are non-distinct. Firm size measured in *log(Total assets)* reduces the *Equity ratio* across all examined samples.

Table 14

DiD – The impact of success on the equity ratio for different samples, posttreatment period 3 years

	(1) All firms	(2) All SMEs	(3) All firms with GPP CA	(4) All SMEs with GPP CA
Treatment effect	-0.0188**	-0.0135	-0.0239*	-0.0103
	(-2.41)	(-1.49)	(-1.68)	(-0.72)
Posttreatment period	0.00420	0.00613	-0.00823	0.000542
	(0.56)	(0.71)	(-1.03)	(0.06)
log(Total Assets)	-0.0505***	-0.0437***	-0.0463***	-0.0399***
	(-7.54)	(-5.32)	(-5.22)	(-3.50)
Constant	1.144***	1.002***	1.064***	0.935***
	(10.22)	(7.56)	(7.27)	(5.13)
Year Dummies	YES	YES	YES	YES
Country Dummies	YES	YES	YES	YES
Industry Dummies	YES	YES	YES	YES
Observations	12350	8172	7234	4855
R^2	0.066	0.059	0.070	0.067
# Firms	1382	1111	786	642

t statistics in parentheses, * $p < 0.10$, ** $p < 0.05$, *** $p < 0.01$

Table 15 presents the DiD models' results for the effect of the CA on the short-term debt ratio (*STDB ratio*). The *Treatment effect* shows mainly insignificant coefficients. In comparison to the peer group, the successful firms do not take on higher nor lower short-term debt ratios. The only exceptions are SMEs with success in a GPP tender. For those firms CA success leads to a lower *STDB ratio* in the post treatment period than that of non-treated firms in the control group. This finding may on the one hand indicate that those successful green firms are capable of lowering their short-term debt share in the years after the award. On the other hand, it could point to banks' inability to recognize green SMEs' success, as those firms are not allowed a higher short-term debt share even if they have been successful in a GPP. Firm size significantly increases the short-term debt ratio. Overall, similar to Hypothesis 1, we can confirm Hypothesis 2. Success in a PP affects the successful firm's future financial strength, but the effect is observed only for some types of firms and Public Procurement procedures.

Table 15

DiD – The impact of success on the STDB ratio for different samples, posttreatment period 3 years

	(1) All firms	(2) All SMEs	(3) All firms with GPP CA	(4) All SMEs with GPP CA
Treatment effect	0.00482	-0.00386	-0.0217	-0.0273*
	(0.60)	(-0.40)	(-1.43)	(-1.87)
Posttreatment period	-0.00807	0.00678	0.0109	0.0228**
	(-1.02)	(0.72)	(1.28)	(2.21)
log(Total Assets)	0.0433***	0.0453***	0.0436***	0.0408***
	(6.60)	(5.38)	(6.12)	(3.99)
Constant	-0.476***	-0.454***	-0.470***	-0.368**
	(-4.34)	(-3.34)	(-3.99)	(-2.25)
Year Dummies	YES	YES	YES	YES
Country Dummies	YES	YES	YES	YES
Industry Dummies	YES	YES	YES	YES
Observations	12002	7965	7034	4728
R^2	0.035	0.034	0.041	0.039
# Firms	1378	1098	784	633

t statistics in parentheses, * $p < 0.10$, ** $p < 0.05$, *** $p < 0.01$

Conclusions

The study tackles the question of whether the financial strength of firms winning PP contract awards, conditional on their SME status, is causally linked to the procurement of contracts from local governments and municipalities. We focus in particular on the procurement of RES contracts. The basis for the analysis is a combined dataset of the Tenders Electronic Daily (TED) 2015–2018 and the AMADEUS firm database covering the 10 European countries under investigation in the XPRESS project. The dataset consists of TED (treated) firms and matched control firms which did not receive a CA but are similar to the treated firms. According to *The Common Procurement*

Vocabulary (CPV) the majority of observed contracts are either in the Green Public Procurement segment or in the "green possible" Public Procurement segment.

We structure the analysis along two main research hypotheses: first, the likelihood of winning a public procurement tender is affected by a firm's financial strength, and second, the impact of winning a public procurement award benefits a firm's future financial strength. To capture the impact of financial strength on the winning chance we apply probit models to samples of successful firms and control firms. To test the causal effect of receiving a contract award on the firm's financial strength we apply the flexpanel DiD approach.

The probit models' estimation results show that the equity ratio has a significant and negative impact on the chance to win a tender. A lower equity ratio increases the likelihood to be successful in a PP tender. One explanation could be that the equity-rich companies might fall victim of the "fat cat" syndrome and exert less effort to be successful in public procurements compared with expanding firms with low equity ratios, as a low equity ratio is a typical characteristic of quickly expanding firms. Fast growing firms are also often fairly young firms. Accordingly, the firms' equity ratios could be a proxy for firm age. If public authorities systematically favored younger firms in the tender process to foster economic growth, the link between a firm's low equity ratio and its success in the public tender would reflect the preferences of the award granting authorities. We cannot entirely rule out this explanation since we cannot control for firm age. However, the rules under which a contract award is granted are very strict and rarely leave room for authorities to follow their own preferences. For this reason, we favor the explanation that the firms' effort makes the difference. Firms with low equity ratios are usually more financially constrained and are more in need of funds and liquidity that accompany a contract award. The short-term debt ratio has a significant and positive effect on winning a tender. Firms with higher short-term debt ratios are more likely to win tenders. The effect may again reflect the high liquidity needs of expanding firms. Those firms may be more willing to heavily engage in winning public procurement tenders.

When analyzing the causal impact of winning a contract award on the firms' financial strength, we focus on the equity ratio and the short-term debt ratio. We find that success lowers the equity ratio of the successful firms in the years after the success no matter whether the firm receives a traditional or a GPP contract. In contrast, we only find an impact of contract awards on the short-term debt ratio in the sample of SMEs receiving a GPP contract. In summary, the DiD analysis provides evidence that receiving an award allows those firms to work with low equity ratios. This may indicate that the award is a substitute for a high equity ratio and, thus, works in favor of improving the firm's access to debt financing after receiving an award.

Green public procurement gains increasingly more attention in the discussion on how governments can support the Great Green Transition. Our study is a contribution to the still small but growing research on the question of whether green public procurement is relevant for a firm's finances. We have shown that firms with low equity ratios are at an advantage in competing for a public tender. In addition, we find that award-winning firms maintain low equity ratios after winning a contract award. We interpret these findings as a sign that financial institutions are prepared to tolerate low equity ratios as the contract award signals creditworthiness.

Our study is only a first step in examining the role of green public procurement for implementing climate-protecting products and services. To make further progress in this respect better data are necessary. A clear labeling of tenders either as compatible or incompatible with the EU Green Deal and, thus, GPP goods, services and works would avoid any ambiguity and support green innovation. In addition, an easier identification of those tenders that qualify for public promotion and, thus, can be financed by issuing sovereign green bonds would most likely support the development of a strong and highly liquid market for sovereign green bonds, and also facilitate the prevention of "greenwashing".

References

— Aghion, P., R. Veugelers, and D. Hemous (2009): *No green growth without innovation.* Bruegel Policy Brief, 2009/07.
— Appelt, S. and F. Galindo-Rueda (2016): *Measuring the Link between Public Procurement and Innovation.* OECD Science, Technology and Industry Working Papers, 2016/03. OECD Publishing, Paris. http://dx.doi.org/10.1787/5jlvc7sl1w7h-en.
— Aschhoff, B. and W. Sofka (2009): *Innovation on demand – Can public procurement drive market success of innovations?* Research policy, 38(8), 1235–1247.
— Bareinboim, E. and J. Pearl (2016): *Causal inference and the data-fusion problem,* Proceedings of the National Academy of Sciences of the United States of America 113(27), 7345–7352.
— Brown, J., G. Martinsson, and B. Petersen, B. (2012): *Do financing constraints matter for R&D?* European Economic Review 56(8), 1512–1529.
— Cecere, G., N. Corrocher, C. Gossart, and M. Ozman (2014a): *Lock-in and path dependence: an evolutionary approach to eco-innovations.* Journal of Evolutionary Economics 24(5), 1037–1065.
— Cecere, G., N. Corrocher, C. Gossart, and M. Ozman (2014b): *Patterns of Innovation in Green ICT: A Patent-Based Analysis.* Published in G. Cecere, N. Corrocher, C. Gossart, and M. Ozman, 2014. Technological pervasiveness and variety of innovators in Green ICT: A patent-based analysis. Research Policy 43, 1827–1839.
— Cheng, W., A. Appolloni, A. D'Amato, and W. Zhu (2018): *Green Public Procurement, missing concepts and future trends – A critical review.* Journal of Cleaner Production 176, 770–784.
— COM (2008): *Public procurement for a better environment.* Brussels. COM(2008) 400 final.
— Cosci, S., V. Meliciani, and V. Sabato (2016): *Relationship lending and innovation: empirical evidence on a sample of European firms.* Economics of Innovation and New Technology, 25(4), 335–357.
— Czarnitzki, D., P. Hünermund, and N. Moshgbar (2018): *Public procurement as policy instrument for innovation.* ZEW-Centre for European Economic Research Discussion Paper, (18–001).
— De Marchi, V. (2012): *Environmental innovation and R&D cooperation: Empirical evidence from Spanish manufacturing firms.* Research policy 41(3), 614–623.
— Dettmann, E., A. Giebler, and A. Weyh (2020): *Flexpaneldid: A Stata toolbox for causal analysis with varying treatment time and duration.* IWH Discussion Papers (3/2020).
— European Commission (2019). *Public procurement indicators 2017.* Brussels, DG GROW.
— Fazekas, M. and B. Tóth (2017): *The Effectiveness of the European Union in Safeguarding Competition in Public Procurement Markets.* SSRN Electronic Journal. 10.2139/ssrn.3101885.
— Ghisetti, C. (2017): *Demand-pull and environmental innovations: Estimating the effects of innovative public procurement.* Technological Forecasting and Social Change, 125, 178–187.
— Ghisetti, C., S. Mancinelli, M. Mazzanti, and M. Zoli (2017): *Financial barriers and environmental innovations: evidence from EU manufacturing firms.* Climate Policy 17(sup1), 131–147.

— Hall, B., P. Moncada-Paternò-Castello, S. Montresor, and A. Vezzani (2016): *Financing constraints, R&D investments and innovative performances: new empirical evidence at the firm level for Europe.* Economics of Innovation and New Technology. 25. 1–14. 10.1080/10438599.2015.1076194.
— Hottenrott, H. and B. Peters (2012): *Innovative capability and financing constraints for innovation: more money, more innovation?* Review of Economics and Statistics 94(4), 1126–1142.
— Hünermund, P. and D. Czarnitzki (2019): Innovation Policy and Causality. ifo DICE Report, 17(04), 3–6.
— Jensen, F., D. Schäfer, and A. Stephan (2019): Financial Constraints of Firms with Environmental Innovation, Vierteljahrshefte zur Wirtschaftsforschung/Quarterly Journal of Economic Research, DIW Berlin, German Institute for Economic Research, vol. 88(3), 43–65. https://ideas.repec.org/a/diw/diwvjh/88-3-3.html.
— Kemfert, C., D. Schäfer and W. Semmler (2020): *Great green transition and finance.* Intereconomics, 55, 181–186.
— Kemp, R. and V. Oltra (2011): *Research insights and challenges on eco-innovation dynamics, Industry and Innovation.* 18(03), 249–253.
— King, G. (2019): *Simplifying Matching Methods for Causal Inference,* Institute for Quantitative Social Science, Harvard University (Presentation Slides).
— Larson, S. and A. Picou (2002): *The market's response to contract award announcements: government versus corporate contracts.* Journal of Public Procurement.
— Myers, S. and N. Majluf (1984): *Corporate financing and investment decisions when firms have information that investors do not have.* Journal of financial economics 13(2), 187–221.
— Olmos, L., S. Ruester, and S. Liong (2012): *On the selection of financing instruments to push the development of new technologies: Application to clean energy technologies.* Energy Policy 43, 252–266.
— Rennings, K. (2000): *Redefining innovation – eco-innovation research and the contribution from ecological economics.* Ecological economics 32(2), 319–332.
— Schäfer, D., A. Stephan, and J. Mosquera (2017): *Family ownership: does it matter for funding and success of corporate innovations?* Small Business Economics 48(4), 931–951. https://doi.org/10.1007/s11187-016-9813-y.
— Wulandari, F., D. Schäfer, A. Stephan, and S. Chen (2018): *The impact of liquidity risk on the yield spread of green bonds.* Finance Research Letters 27, 53–59. https://doi.org/10.1016/j.frl.2018.02.025.
— Zipperer, V. (2019): *Green public procurement and the innovation activities of firms.* DIW discussion paper.

Appendix 1: Tender Types

CODE SELECTION	SHORT CODE SELECTION		Type of tender (1 = GPP, 2 = GPP possible, 3 = Brown tender)
31121300-3	31121300	Wind-energy generators	1
31121310-6	31121310	Windmills	3
31121320-9	31121320	Wind turbines	1
31121330-2	31121330	Wind turbine generators	1
31121331-9	31121331	Turbine rotors	2
31121340-5	31121340	Wind farm	1

Continued

CODE SELECTION	SHORT CODE SELECTION		Type of tender (1 = GPP, 2 = GPP possible, 3 = Brown tender)
38126400-8	38126400	Wind surface observing apparatus	3
45251160-0	45251160	Wind-power installation works	1
09300000-2	9300000	Electricity, heating, solar and nuclear energy	1
09330000-1	9330000	Solar energy	1
09331000-8	9331000	Solar panels	1
09331100-9	9331100	Solar collectors for heat production	1
09331200-0	9331200	Solar photovoltaic modules	1
09332000-5	9332000	Solar installation	1
31712347-4	31712347	Power or solar diodes	2
38126200-6	38126200	Solar radiation surface observing apparatus	3
45261215-4	45261215	Solar panel roof-covering work	1
31712331-9	31712331	Photovoltaic cells	1
45251120-8	45251120	Hydro-electric plant construction work	1
45251140-4	45251140	Thermal power plant construction work	3
45251141-1	45251141	Geothermal power station construction work	1
45248000-7	45248000	Construction work for hydro-mechanical structures	3
42511110-5	42511110	Heat pumps	1
42530000-0	42530000	Parts of refrigerating and freezing equipment and heat pumps	1
42533000-1	42533000	Parts of heat pumps	1
09134230-8	9134230	Biodiesel	1
09134231-5	9134231	Biodiesel (B20)	1
09134232-2	9134232	Biodiesel (B100)	1
31124000-1	31124000	Steam-turbine generator and related apparatus	2
42112100-8	42112100	Steam turbines	3
42112200-9	42112200	Hydraulic turbines	3
42113100-5	42113100	Parts of steam turbines	3
51130000-2	51130000	Installation services of steam generators, turbines, compressors and burners	3
42113200-6	42113200	Parts of hydraulic turbines	3
42112210-2	42112210	Water wheels	3
42113400-8	42113400	Parts of water wheels	3
42121000-3	42121000	Hydraulic or pneumatic power engines and motors	2
42121100-4	42121100	Hydraulic or pneumatic cylinders	2
42121200-5	42121200	Hydraulic power engines	2
42121400-7	42121400	Hydraulic power motors	2
42122210-5	42122210	Hydraulic power packs	2
42124150-0	42124150	Parts of hydraulic power engines or motors	2
42124221-9	42124221	Parts of hydraulic power packs	2
09111400-4	9111400	Wood fuels	1
03416000-9	3416000	Wood waste	1
03413000-8	3413000	Fuel wood	1
24327200-4	24327200	Wood charcoal	3
45251142-8	45251142	Wood-fired power station construction work	1

Continued

CODE SELECTION	SHORT CODE SELECTION		Type of tender (1 = GPP, 2 = GPP possible, 3 = Brown tender)
34144900-7	34144900	Electric vehicles	1
34144910-0	34144910	Electric buses	1
51111000-3	51111000	Installation services of electric motors, generators and transformers	2
51111100-4	51111100	Installation services of electric motors	2
31100000-7	31100000	Electric motors, generators and transformers	2
31110000-0	31110000	Electric motors	2
31160000-5	31160000	Parts of electric motors, generators and transformers	2
31161000-2	31161000	Parts for electrical motors and generators	2
50532100-4	50532100	Repair and maintenance services of electric motors	2
71314000-2	71314000	Energy and related services	2
65400000-7	65400000	Other sources of energy supplies and distribution	2
09000000-3	9000000	Petroleum products, fuel, electricity and other sources of energy	2
09310000-5	9310000	Electricity	2
31200000-8	31200000	Electricity distribution and control apparatus	2
31682000-0	31682000	Electricity supplies	2
24111600-1	24111600	Hydrogen	2
09323000-9	9323000	District heating	2
42515000-9	42515000	District heating boiler	3
45251250-8	45251250	District-heating plant construction work	3
45232140-5	45232140	District-heating mains construction work	3
42320000-5	42320000	Waste incinerators	2
45252300-1	45252300	Refuse-incineration plant construction work	3
51135110-1	51135110	Installation services of waste incinerators	2
90513300-9	90513300	Refuse incineration services	3

AUTHORS

Christopher F. Baum is Professor of Economics and Social Work at Boston College, where he presently serves as Chair of the Department of Economics. He is a Research Fellow in the Department of Macroeconomics, German Institute for Economic Research, and an Associate Researcher at the Centre of Excellence for Science and Innovation Studies (CESIS) in Stockholm. He has coauthored several statistical software routines in the Stata language and three books about Stata. He earned the Ph.D. in Economics at the University of Michigan – Ann Arbor. His current research focuses on labor market outcomes of refugee immigrants and several public health topics relating to substance use, environmental impacts on birth outcomes, and mental health impacts of the pandemic.

Janina Bösche is a Research Associate at the School of International Business Bremen. She studied Business Law and Business Administration in Osnabrück and Hamburg. Since 2021 she works on her dissertation in cooperation with the University of Bremen. Her research focuses on sustainable finance and behavioral finance.

Sabrina Hegner is Professor for International Management at the School of International Business of the Hochschule Bremen. She holds a Master degree in Psychology from the University of Mannheim (Germany) as well as a Master degree in Business from the University of Western Sydney (Australia) and a Ph.D. in Brand Management from the University of Bremen. Her major research interest is in consumer psychology and cross-cultural research.

Arash Kordestani is Assistant Professor of Logistics at Södertörn University, Stockholm. He received his Ph.D. from Lulea University of Technology, Sweden. He does research in Business Administration field, and in recent years, his main research themes have been shaped around blockchain, circular economy, machine learning, sustainable supply chains, and public procurement.

Katharina Riebe graduated in Economics at the University of Bremen. She is a Research Associate at the Media Competence Center (MMCC) of the City University of Applied Sciences Bremen. She is responsible for digitization in the teaching-learning context and electronic assessments. Her research focuses on determinants of learning success, literacy, economics of education and gender-specific aspects.

Dorothea Schäfer, Research Director Financial Markets at DIW Berlin and Adjunct Professor at Jönköping University – JIBS (Economics). She achieved her Ph.D. and habilitation at the FU Berlin. Schäfer has been head of various research projects funded e. g. by the German Research Foundation (DFG), the EU Commission and the research arm of the DSGV (German Savings Bank Association). She has published in Journal of International Financial Markets, Institutions & Money, International Journal of Money and Finance, European Journal of Finance, Small Business Economics, Journal of Financial Stability and many other journals. She was an expert for many committees, e. g. the Bundestag's Committee on Finance. She is Editor-in-Chief of Vierteljahrshefte zur Wirtschaftsforschung and of the Eurasian Economic Review (EAER).

Mechthild Schrooten has been working as a Professor at the School of International Business, Hochschule Bremen since 2007. Before, she was a Senior Researcher and Deputy Head of Department "International Economics" at the DIW Berlin and a Professor at the Hitotsubashi University, Tokyo. Today as before, her main fields of interest are transformations, tension and extreme events in international economics. She is a founder of the research Cluster DTX (dynamics, tension and xtreme events) at Hochschule Bremen. Recently, she is publishing on banking, sustainable finance and macroeconomic stability in uncertain times. She holds a doctorate degree from the Free University Berlin.

Andreas Stephan is Professor of Forest Industrial Economics at Linnaeus University, Sweden; and has been a Professor of Economics and Finance at Jönköping International Business School, Sweden. He graduated with a M.Sc. in Industrial Engineering from Technical University in Berlin and earned a Ph.D. in Economics at Humboldt University Berlin. He previously held positions at the Social Science Research Center Berlin (WZB), at the German Institute for Economic Research (DIW) and at the European University Viadrina. He is a Research Affiliate with CESIS – Centre of Excellence for Science and Innovation Studies at the Royal Institute of Technology in Stockholm. Andreas Stephan's research interests are related to climate and forest policies, ESG and financial markets, and green investment and finance. He is an appointed Associate Editor for the journal Eurasian Economic Review and Editorial Board Member for the journals Business Strategy and the Environment.

Armin Varmaz is Professor for International Finance at the School of International Business Bremen. Previously, he was a Research Assistant at the University of Bremen, a Visiting Researcher at Brown University, NKU, Harvard University and a Professor of Finance at the University of Freiburg. He earned the doctorate (2006) and habilitation (2017) at the University of Bremen. His research and work interests include asset pricing, sustainable finance, portfolio management and asset allocation, empirical capital market research and computational finance. He is author of numerous articles in well-recognized international journals and of the books "Equity Valuation: Models from Leading Investment Banks", "Computational Finance" and "Matlab for students and professionals".

Table of contents 2021

DANK AN DIE GUTACHTERINNEN UND GUTACHTER

Die Redaktion der „Vierteljahrshefte zur Wirtschaftsforschung" dankt den Heftherausgeberinnen und -herausgebern und den weiteren Gutachterinnen und Gutachtern, die im Jahr 2021 die eingereichten Manuskripte beurteilt haben. Der Begutachtungsprozess (Peer Review Verfahren) wurde von den Herausgeberinnen und Herausgebern organisiert, die auch ergänzende Gutachten erstellt haben.

A THANK YOU TO THE REFEREES

The Editorial Board of the „Quarterly Journal of Economic Research" would like to thank the editors of the respective journal issues and all other referees who have given their reviews on manuscripts submitted to the journal in 2021. The peer review process was organized by the editors, who also delivered additional reviewer reports.

Heft 1/2021

Lukas Menkhoff, Deutsches Institut für Wirtschaftsforschung DIW Berlin
Doris Neuberger, Universität Rostock

Heft 2/2021

Horst Gischer, Otto-von-Guericke Universität Magdeburg
Bernhard Herz, Universität Bayreuth
Christoph Kaserer, Technische Universität München
Dorothea Schäfer, DIW Berlin

Heft 3/2021

Horst Gischer, Otto-von-Guericke Universität Magdeburg
Bernhard Herz, Universität Bayreuth
Christoph Kaserer, Technische Universität München
Dorothea Schäfer, DIW Berlin

Heft 4/2021

Mechthild Schrooten, University of Applied Sciences Bremen
Armin Varmaz, Bremen University, University of Applied Sciences Bremen
Dorothea Schäfer, German Institute for Economic Research, DIW Berlin

HINWEISE FÜR AUTORINNEN UND AUTOREN DER VIERTELJAHRSHEFTE

Die Vierteljahrshefte zur Wirtschaftsforschung sind die älteste Publikation des DIW Berlin, sie erscheinen bereits seit 1926. Angesammeltes ForscherInnen- und ExpertInnenwissen wird auf wirtschaftspolitische Probleme angewandt. Das DIW Vierteljahrsheft bringt Praktikerinnen und Praktiker aus Wirtschaft und Politik mit Wissenschaftlerinnen und Wissenschaftlern am DIW Berlin und weit darüber hinaus zusammen. Jedes Heft greift ein aktuelles Thema aus der Wirtschaftspolitik auf. So bietet die Zeitschrift wichtige Orientierungshilfe zu komplexen wirtschaftspolitischen Themen und zeigt neue Perspektiven und Lösungsvorschläge auf.

Alle Beiträge werden begutachtet. Die Themen der nächsten Schwerpunkthefte und ausführliche Hinweise für Autorinnen und Autoren können der DIW-Internetseite entnommen werden (www.diw.de). Beiträge sind an die Redaktion und an die Heftverantwortlichen einzusenden. Berücksichtigt werden nur Originalbeiträge, die im Falle der Annahme auch tatsächlich zur Veröffentlichung in den Vierteljahrsheften zur Verfügung stehen.

Die Beiträge können in deutscher und in englischer Sprache eingereicht werden. Eine Zusammenfassung des Beitrags ist in deutscher und in englischer Sprache gesondert zu erstellen. Diese soll jeweils nicht mehr als 150 Wörter umfassen. Außerdem müssen dem Manuskript mindestens drei Begriffe der JEL-Klassifikation (www.aeaweb.org/journal/jel_class_system.html) und mindestens drei englischsprachige Keywords beigefügt werden. Neben dem Regelfall des deutschsprachigen Heftes sind auch Vierteljahrshefte in englischer Sprache möglich, wenn die Themenstellung dies nahelegt. Vierteljahrshefte mit sowohl deutsch- als auch englischsprachigen Beiträgen sind ebenfalls möglich.

Das Manuskript ist in Schriftgröße 12 pt im Zeilenabstand von 1,5 zu erstellen und mit einem linken und rechten Rand von 2,5 cm zu versehen. Der Umfang des Manuskripts sollte 15 Seiten (circa 30 000 Zeichen, ohne Tabellen und Abbildungen) nicht überschreiten. Die Zitierweise ist den Aufsätzen des Vierteljahrsheftes zu entnehmen.

Der Textteil ist in MS Word zu liefern. Tabellen und Abbildungen sind als separate Dateien zu liefern (Tabellen in MS Excel, Abbildungen zusammen mit den zugrunde liegenden Daten – entweder ebenfalls in Excel oder einem anderen gängigen Vektor-Grafikformat, vorzugsweise eps). Alle Abbildungen müssen in Graustufen (s/w) und in reproduktionsfähiger Form vorliegen (Bilder mit mind. 300 dpi. Abbildungen mit grafischen Elementen, z.B. mit Text oder Linien, mind. 600 dpi). Die Stellen, an denen sie im Text erscheinen sollen, müssen im Manuskript markiert werden. Die maximale Breite von Tabellen und Abbildungen beträgt 12,6 cm. Bei Tabellen die Zeilen- und Spaltenmerkmale bitte übersichtlich aufteilen. Anmerkungen und Fußnoten sowie Quellenangabe(n) bitte unter dem Tabellenfeld beziehungsweise der Grafik positionieren.

Wichtiger Hinweis: Falls Sie Abbildungen oder Ähnliches aus dem Internet entnehmen, bitten wir um Mitlieferung einer Kopie der Druckgenehmigung. Auch hier ist auf eine entsprechende Auflösung (s.o., nicht interpoliert) zu achten.

Für die im Vierteljahrsheft erscheinenden Artikel gilt eine einjährige Sperrfrist, erst danach sind die Artikel frei zugänglich